Pathway Teachings
Question and Answer Series

GW00692028

Pathway Teachings

by

Red Feather

(Via the mediumship of Joy Foubister)

Regency Press (London & New York) Ltd.
125 High Holborn, London WC1V 6QA

Copyright © 1989 by Joy Foubister

This book is copyrighted under the Berne Convention.
No portion may be reproduced by any process without
the copyright holder's written permission except for the
purposes of reviewing or criticism, as permitted under
the Copyright Act of 1956.

ISBN 0 7212 0875 4

Printed and bound in Great Britain by
Buckland Press Ltd., Dover, Kent.

Dedication

To my husband, Kenny, for his patient support and to Anne, Doreen and Mary for allowing me to share their gift of true friendship.

Index

Question 1

Anne:–How did spirit originate?

Red Feather:– You have not as yet the full consciousness to take in the depth which this question deserves. I will try to bring it to a level which will give you understanding though it will not be a full answer – that can only come with your increased understanding.

In the beginning there was consciousness, that consciousness through time perpetuated itself into motion and came forward. The motion then became activated into spiritual activity, into being. At this point this spirit in being was untested, pure but untested. There had to occur a situation where experience could bring about the testing of this untried spirit.

From this beginning comes all experiences to help us understand the initial spirit being which is of ourselves, but this time with strength. Experiences are given to every spirit being in a variety of ways. There are experiences for the spirit which cannot be given from earth, but equally, there are other experiences which only the earth situation can give to spirit. You must understand that a spirit being as a whole must have all experiences, both of the earth and not of the earth. You at this time are experiencing those of the earth with no recollection of those previously experienced elsewhere.

As you raise consciousness within yourself, you raise the availability to bring the strength gained from previous experiences elsewhere to add to experiences gained upon earth. You must understand that this takes a long, long time, because the strength and understanding of each spirit being varies.

Two individual spirit beings experiencing the same strengthening process will derive different strengths from that experience and therefore progress at different rates. This is why you have upon your earth so many different people at different stages of development. The experience may be the same, but the strength required and absorbed, or understood, is different for each spirit – therefore the strength gained is different.

The higher you raise your spirit consciousness through experiences gained here and elsewhere the stronger your spirit becomes, the stronger the push forward to gain the pure strength which your spirit consciousness wishes. Those who feel within them the pull and push and the draw of the one you call God, are in the process of raising their spirit consciousness, of strengthening the spirit consciousness, because they have re-established through past experiences here and elsewhere that this is the link required by them. They recognise as a child recognises a parent that this is where the guidance and help will come from.

This answer but a brief and simple explanation in response to a complex question.

Anne:–Please explain Universal Consciousness. Is it individual consciousness all put together?

Red Feather:–Within universal consciousness there is individual consciousness. Both degrees of consciousness require strengthening. The way this is done is for each individual consciousness to realise within itself the way it needs to be strengthened to become a greater part of the whole. In this way the God force – universal consciousness – is strengthened through the individual consciousness and is therefore itself strengthened.

The individual consciousness knows what it needs to attain and therefore sets out on a progressive journey of self-discovery unfolding higher and higher levels as it seeks its source of purity.

Anne:–I have wondered if all spirits had had to make their way through the darkness into the light.

Red Feather:–All spirit beings do not necessarily need darkness to give them the experience required, some spirits from the very beginning have been able to link to this consciousness. They have always known and understood that it is there, and have been able to respond to the best within them – therefore they did not need to experience the darkness.

Anne:–Are those the ones who never required to come to earth?

Red Feather:–Some of them have been to the earth. There is more good in your world than is given credit. The souls that are good are rarely recognised by those on earth, only usually by us. Therefore the good that they do is recognised by spirit in general and by the individual spirit concerned. They do not have to experience the throes of darkness to know that the darkness is wrong. If you have within the link to the God force you will create your own light in that darkness and gain strength through your experience; for as you recognise your own darkness (ignorance) you gain knowledge of spiritual worth.

Although the world in general appears, from where you stand, to be covered in darkness – this is not so. There are densities of darkness and your appreciation of darkness is limited. There are some situations upon your earth which are evil – absolute darkness, they need the light of the earth to work out their experiences to find their own link to strengthen their own spirit being and bring a more enlightened understanding to bear. This will be done.

There are also situations in the world that appear as darkness but in fact are little flickers of light. By this I mean those in the darker situations are struggling and finding their own higher consciousness and through that link they will pull themselves out of their ignorance into greater understanding, thus alleviating the darkness for themselves and for those around them.

Question 2

Anne asked Red Feather about freedom of her spirit. She had been told twice before that her spirit had known freedom; if this was so – how then was she now in difficulty trying to reach a vibration rate so that she could again 'converse with spirit' as a free spirit?

Red Feather:–You are confusing values of freedom. The freedom you have in spirit is far greater than that you bring down to earth. When you once again take on the cloak of mortality it is as if the density of that freedom becomes less palpable. The freedom is the same, its use is different due to the cloak of mortality as against the cloak of immortality.

There are different stages of freedom which you can earn; you are allowed the freedom carried by previous service and understanding – within that range you always have freedom. When you come to earth with that degree of freedom you are presented with a choice of circumstances through which to express that freedom in a responsible way and thereby gain an added degree of progression as spirit.

Your freedom degree is the strength which propels you through earthly life. That freedom can be added to whilst you are upon earth by using and finding the spirit within to unlock the vibrational level already gained. Once the need for harmony of body and soul is recognised your physical life becomes strengthened, more purposeful and broadens out to give greater opportunity to the expanding spirit. The more in mortal life you strengthen that link with your own spirit freedom the greater the gain of the soul.

You cannot lose the degree of spirit freedom gained before you came to earth, but through refusing to learn the lessons life presents you lose the possible gain available for this lifetime.

Anne asks why she is having such a struggle to free the spirit now, when she has been told the spirit has been free before.

Red Feather:–Your struggle is not in trying to free spirit but in trying to find the vibrational link to that key. Everyone's spirit is free within its own vibrational level but when you come to earth to gain greater freedom and knowledge of who you are, you must re-establish that link. You must do this on your own through trial and error – no one else can do it for you.

You find it difficult because you have been conditioned by earthly life and thinking with its lack of understanding yourselves as spirit and from which you are now trying to gain freedom.

All, during mortal life, have accepted ideas and practises given to them by others but you have come to a point of knowing that those ideas do not hold the whole truth for you and that there must be something more – you were not clearly aware of what that 'more' was and this you are in the process of now discovering.

Anne:–Trying to unlock the vibrational level, is that where the affinity comes in?

Red Feather: The vibrational level is the physical receptive influence of the spiritual affinity; it is where the glimmering of spirit purpose is felt in the more dense atmosphere of earth. To walk truly as spirit you must walk on an affinity level which is higher than a vibrational level. At present you are still walking upon the vibrational level to gain further insight into your soul need. In this way will you progress and earn for yourselves more freedom and responsibility of spirit. In your lives on earth you should recognise this growing awareness taking place by the harmony of body and soul working together to further your understanding and love of all mankind.

Anne:–The growing awareness being as a child hearing of the teachings of Jesus, but not really understanding the true significance?

Red Feather:–Yes, but learning to understand and follow in the true way. To use your analogy – you must understand that the idea of Jesus is a good one, the difficulty lies in man's understanding of those ideas. You are beginning to relate to the true Christ consciousness, the true reason why Jesus came to earth, and in that way you expand freedom to accept newer ideas which will add to the feeling and knowledge already held.

The point of freedom of spirit is to expand yourselves to encompass the truth of God as given by the God feeling inside you, not as the God truths propounded by any other person. You must find the God truth for the self, within the self, other people can suggest ideas to you but unless you find that truth within it has no value.

To gain freedom in spirit is to use more of that inner feeling for the good of other people as a natural expression of your life; it is not the knocking down of barriers, it is the opening up of the self to this God feeling within so that when you return once again to spirit you have managed to absorb more of the truth of God and thereby gained more spiritual freedom through natural progression.

Question 3

Anne:–Earth has periods of light and darkness (day and night). Is this because earth is the borderland between the spheres of dark and the spheres of light?

Red Feather:–You must not confuse areas of spirituality with those required through the balance of nature. Your earth is divided into two periods – light and darkness (day and night) bringing benefit to the balance of nature and all who are within the earth's surface and draw. In the spirit world we have no light and darkness as such, there is no need for it, the vibrational range separates light from dark.

On your earth you are living in a mortal body physically constructed for physical life upon the earth. That physical body requires certain conditions in which to thrive and to grow.

In daylight is the thriving time – the forging ahead time. The light from the rays of your sun and of your atmosphere bring to the physical body certain components which it needs to fulfil physical work upon your earth. Conversely the darkness brings the closing down of this and opening of the inner person so that the physical body rests. The components which it had during the daylight hours are no longer there, instead the spiritual atmosphere comes through in this quieter atmosphere to penetrate into physical states of body and of mind.

You need the two to have complete balance otherwise the physical body would not be able to withstand the strain upon it, you need the darkness to have this period of physical rest. Plants, birds, animals, are constructed in the same way, they take from either the night or the day the attributes which are necessary for their physical life upon a physical world.

Anne:–Many people upon the earth are afraid of the darkness. Is it because we have come from the darkness, and realise within the subconscious mind the things of the darkness?

Red Feather:–The fear of the darkness in many is a fear subconsciously of opening themselves to spirit. They are aware of a subtle inner response but because they do not understand or do not wish to understand a fear is created by the unknown. This brings about a fear of physical darkness. It is not physical darkness they are afraid of – it is spiritual darkness.

Anne:–I have always thought Jesus Christ was one spirit. Something I have read recently now makes me unsure. Was Christ the affinity of

Jesus, Jesus the medium of Christ?

Red Feather:–Jesus is the manifestation of the Christ consciousness, part of the whole consciousness. There have been many such as Jesus; there will be many such as Jesus, but in a different form. There will never again be someone who will have the impact of Jesus upon your part of the world. Your world needed him at that time to take it forward; unfortunately, part of this mission has been subverted by man's mind, man's interpretation of His work. Until this has been corrected there will not be again another such as the Jesus manifestation of the Christ consciousness.

Anne:–Speaking from my own experience of this, the more one tries to become spiritual, the more one tries to utilise the spiritual self, the less control one appears to have of the mind. Its thoughts often not being in union with that you are trying to achieve and do. It throws up obstructions if you will – thoughts which are unspiritual, negative, impure.

Red Feather:–You are so impatient, my little one. You cannot force spirituality, it has to come through a natural growth of the self. This does not mean to say that you must not try to achieve spirituality. You do this by gaining understanding, seeking and searching within yourself to find this understanding.

This process has to be done slowly and naturally to bring about a gentle balance. To have you searching for spirituality one week and finding it the next would create imbalance within the evolving spirit; it must be done so that spirituality achieves a natural balance in all paths of your life – both physical and spiritual. That balance is achieved in each person in a different way according to the needs of his/her own progression towards purity.

In all people the distance between the searching and the achieving is an area which contains elements of both; this area will take to the surface of your conscious mind thoughts seemingly unrelated and act as little flaws in the character never seen before because you were not aware of the flaw, now they are simply things passing through out of the subconscious, into the conscious, recognised as such and put out. It is a natural part of balance towards attainment of spirituality the mind streamlining of the important from the unimportant. A throwing out of

thoughts no longer required for your progression, a purifying act.
It will go on through all your life because whilst you are upon the earth you have not attained spirituality; what you can attain is a working understanding of your own level of spirituality. It is not a process which can be hurried.
Don't fall into your age old trap of time. Picture yourself on this earth as a little baby who longs to walk but cannot get his legs to obey. This is the stage you are at my little one; you long to pull yourself up and hold on to whatever will support you, but you cannot sustain that height or balance and you fall down again. As the little child becomes impatient with his own inability to walk you become impatient with your inability to walk spiritually. The progress is the same, the child walks through time – so shall you.

Anne:–I was very surprised to read, Red Feather, that men of earth are the only ones to enter the middle or summerland spheres, that only in the higher realms do others come from other districts and areas of the cosmos.

Red Feather:–As your earth has its own planes of progression so do other worlds, only when the progressions are similar do they come together. You must not be surprised by this. Each area of development has its own vibration not always compatible with others' progression. Each person is placed in the sphere – the earth or some other world – within all is spirit and is accordingly bestowed to give the most benefit towards individual progression.
You have on your earth schools for the under fives, primary, secondary, college and universities, within all of those there are various states of growth according to each understanding. Try to imagine spirit as such. You would not take a kindergarten child and place him in a college or university for his understanding would not be of such. So it is with the spirit world – you are placed where you are spiritually capable of receiving progression for yourself at the best rate. When you leave university you then go into a wider world where you mix with other people who have a university education, or an experience of life comparable to your own, where you can exchange ideas on the same level. So it is within the spirit world – that is where all come together.

Question 4

Anne:–Reading one of Silver Birch's books there was an allusion to a deeper relationship than was understood between himself, Barbanell – his medium, and Barbanell's wife. Again, Francis of Assisi was asked by a man he called, son, if this was used as a term of affection or was there a deeper meaning. The answer was in the affirmative. You have told us of the lines of affinity granted by God. I have wondered if we are all facets of our guides' consciousness, of if indeed, the line of affinity is a facet of some higher spiritual being's consciousness which joins and rejoins before becoming merged into the Universal Consciousness.

Red Feather shows Joy clairvoyantly a never ending string of many different coloured beads, such as one may see strung across a child's pram. As Anne was speaking many coloured beads were passed across, size and shape all alike, the only difference being in the colour. The first bead was pure white, the other colours followed and the last bead – belonging to us – was of a pinky red shade. What would have been the string passing through the beads was instead a light – a delicate silvery white light. It appeared so delicate and fine that you would expect it to snap – but you knew that it was of immense strength, the finer – the stronger.

Red Feather:–Central affinity (the silvery white light) never changes, is constant and strong, is always there giving energy to all the colours. The colour denotes the levels of consciousness which come from pure consciousness down through the degrees of understanding. Where there is true affinity, true purpose, a line of communication is established which grows as time passes and understanding continues.

Affinity grows within itself, upon itself, for itself. Each grain of knowledge gained by any part of that affinity line increases the reception and availability of that knowledge for all the other parts of that chain, no matter if the knowledge gained is at the top, bottom or the centre of the chain. The receptivity of any part of the chain affects the whole for the good and it becomes purer and stronger with each particle of true knowledge.

Let me give you an example:–I receive information on the same affinity level as that which comes to me from those higher up the same affinity level, but as my individual consciousness within the universal consciousness is not as great as those who send on the information it is so refined as to my understanding – enough to stretch it that little bit further but not to put it without the bounds of understanding altogether. I then take my understanding of this truth and take it to your understanding giving it the same treatment as it was given for me. In this way I am raised, in this way I raise you; in this way you will raise others, in this way they in turn will raise others.

An unending chain. There is no end to the chain of true affinity as there is no end to universal consciousness. All affinities are connected, this is the way that the soul finds its own progression, each one like a bauble on a chain, each one progressing along that chain as it so needs and understands.

Universal consciousness is a vast concept for the physical mind, it cannot encompass the width, depth or the versatility of it. It appears to you who are on the earth that separate factions work in different ways to bring about the results for universal consciousness. There is no separation rather a gathering in of those in closer affinity to work on one particular section of universal consciousness through the individual consciousness. In this way all is gathered together, all is extended, all is purified, all is progression towards the Godhead. As one is caused into affinity so one becomes the result of that affinity.

Question 5

Joy:–Sometime past, Ho-San gave us a lecture on colour, the meanings of the different colours as we in this group were to use them. Since starting this new interpretation development with Doreen you have been using these same colours, plus variations in a different way with different meanings coming through. Ho-San did say that he would return to give us a further lecture to help us more easily understand the different shadings of the colours. Can you please comment.

Red Feather:–It is true I have been deepening your appreciation of colour. Ho-San will not return just yet for you do not all work with insight into the colour meaning. To use colour properly there must be spiritual insight. All is not lost – through Joy's learning of colour meaning, so too, you will receive a glimmering, thus bringing forward your own receptivity.

The insight of colour is more important than colour itself. It denotes certain things to the trained eye, but you need perception to make colour understandable. Until your perception levels have reached working levels we cannot bring forward Ho-San's lecture to you. Joy must learn to work with colour, for it will be one of the tools she will use to teach; colour tells all, gives all, it can by its correct use be very beneficial. Its precise use is most important.

Anne:–This question, Red Feather, may have something to do with the previous question answered by you for me. A message to me from White Cloud contained – "she who is of the land of my fathers" – I have never understood this.

(Anne's guide, White Cloud, replies.)

White Cloud:–As we are all sons and daughters of God the Father so, too, are we all brothers and sisters of each other. Time passes and we fulfil our different roles in order to gain further experience of the affinity level previously broached. One must learn what it is to be a father, a mother, a son, a daughter, a sister and a brother. One must have these affinities to complete our own affinity.

In this case I am as a father to you, I guide you from spirit as I am guided by Father – the one called God. We have no earthly connotations of relationships such as brothers and sisters – we have Universal Brotherhood. We must learn to gain for ourselves an all round in personality to appreciate all facets of that personality. And so, my daughter, you are fulfilling your purpose – I guide you from spirit as a father guides and loves his daughter, but we are all children of spirit.

Doreen:–I would like to know why, when looking into a mirror at a distance of 4-5 ft, my face lifts, becoming a golden colour then a translucent blue. This has the effect of making me feel faint. Is there any significance?

Red Feather:–This question is easily answered. It is a situation that is often experienced at the beginning of a development before control of the vibrational level has been established.

What you are experiencing is a separation of the spirit self – awareness from the physical body. While you are separated you see the spiritual colours of your own self – thus the gold and the blue. Those are the affinity colours along which you travel. While so separated (so to speak) you see with the spiritual eye the spiritual you. This appears to give you disharmony as understood by the physical mind because at the time this is occurring you are anchored neither by physical nor in spirit – you are neither one nor the other completely. It is true you are always spirit, but at that time your awareness is heightened and is above that of the simply physical thus cannot be controlled by it. As you gain control of the levels you will be able to be in one or the other as required.

Doreen apologises for asking such a question.

Red Feather:–Never apologise for asking. If you do not ask you do not clear the mind, therefore doubt is left. We are unable then to bring forward the deeper teaching required.

Doreen:–In an auragraph reading just after commencing this training, I was told – 'never to let the fumes steal out of the box'. Could Red Feather enlighten me as to its meaning?

Red Feather:–You have already correctly assumed that the fumes spoken of are to do with that part which has been troubling you over recent months. What are fumes? Imperfect air, imperfect vibrations, bringing stagnation to all around. This is part and parcel of karmic conditions, cause and effect.

By telling you not to remove the lid the lady was telling you to keep it under control – don't let it shoot off on its own. Use the lid to control, lift it as you feel able to deal with it, and in time the lid will fall away unneeded, the box will fall away, there will be nothing left but a deep understanding of and an insight into human beings.

(Note – This answer was given to help Doreen understand the positive and negative aspects of herself over various past lives as shown to her in meditation.)

Doreen:–You have stated that Joy has a service affinity with you. Could you please give me a little information about my affinity.

Red Feather:–*(Joy says he is smiling.)* You have opened Pandora's box, I will allow you a little glimpse inside to try and explain a little for you. You must understand that your training and your development is much more than your mind can cope with at the moment, but your higher self does know of it – this is why I can let you have a little look inside Pandora's box.

You have, through the aeons of time gained a great insight and love of your fellow men, of nature, of all things of God. You have a great feeling for balance and harmony. You want to enhance this for the benefit of others who come that they may have an easier time than you, that they may understand in a natural way the gentleness and the beauty which you know is God. The way you will do this is through colour. The affinity with which you have incarnated is the affinity of the love of mankind, the pure love of God for your fellow men.

You want to extend the use and application of colour, the understanding of colour. In spirit work we all have a colour vibration and a note – a musical note. You have been studying the use of colour for a considerable time both in spirit and now on earth – to learn how colour can be utilised for the benefit of other people; first by understanding themselves and then by using that colour for their own benefit. Each person has a colour vibration as they have a musical note, this is made up of a mix of colours but always there is a predominating colour, one predominating note, which indicates to spirit the vibration level that person has achieved.

You are here then to expand your knowledge of general colour, particular colour use will only come when you pass over once more into spirit. You will find as you begin to work that certain colours will attract you; those to be as your chapter of learning this time around. There are a plethora of colours untouched by you which you won't touch in this lifetime. You spirit teachers have cut down as to your needs to let your understanding grow by use of just a few colours.

Imagine how many colours you can see in your physical state – know that in spirit are a myriad of more colours and realise the Pandora's box you have opened – colour therapy, that colour use must be understood by you in its entirety to your degree of understanding and that knowledge then used to bring harmony within to those who seek the deeper meaning of the self.

Anne:–What affinity level am I on?

Red Feather:–You are on a learning affinity. A gathering to yourself of

all things which pertain to the self and the understanding of that self.
You must learn about yourself for until you do you cannot understand
the depth of teaching needed by you. You are progressing well but it
takes time. This kicking over of the traces is a part of it, throwing out
things which you accepted before but now no longer need and making
room for further growth.

(Anne says she wishes she had been more simple.)

Red Feather:–There is no such thing as a simple soul. Why should you
be different? Everyone has to go through this process – we have all
been through it – you must learn the same control as learnt by all, that
same submission and giving of the self in love to the will of God and
thus joining with Him in complete unity.

Question 6

*Anne asks if Red Feather can tell her why she has such a phobia – a
fear of snakes, never having had dealings with them, and living in this
country which only has one poisonous kind.*

Red Feather:–This is a complex question with two separate parts. One
having a physical connotation that will right itself in time and has to do
with a previous life experience. It was not the fear of snakes, as such,
but the fear which snakes engender that grew like a snake within you –
an experience you buried so deep that it is only now beginning to
surface and uncoil.

The other connotation carried on from the lesson comparing you to a
bucking bronco. You do not like being manipulated or tossed around
without purpose, you do not like being used – either by ideas or by
people, you kick against them. Freedom of the self is born very
strongly within you.

The physical self is never aware clearly of what the higher self
desires; the true message never really comes through in its entirety, it
wraps itself into coils as it comes down the vibrational level, becomes
distorted, and this brings about a fear that the physical self will never
gain the freedom of the higher self. It is a fear of being paralysed in the
sense that a snake would paralyse its victim.

The paralysis of lack of freedom is strong within you; the only way freedom can be gained is through its own self – expression and this you are doing. You are shaking yourself free, beginning to find your real self – instead of allowing ignorance to lead you.

Anne:–I am not sure about this, I need to read and then think.

Red Feather:–If you think deeply about it you will realise that the two fears are interacting upon each other at different levels. One is a fear of constraint because the higher self cannot shake the physical self free to know itself, the other brought about on a physical level from a previous life adverse experience, thus containing the physical fear and blocking its freedom at a higher level of understanding. Thus constraint consolidates the fear on the two different levels.

You are now dealing with the spiritual aspect of this fear by freeing the constraint and making the physical self more amenable to the wishes of the higher self, even through that fear. If your fear is allowed to run amok you will take a long time to gain freedom from the damage to yourself, but with spirit help you will gain your freedom through a deeper understanding of its roots.

The physical fear you have of snakes is similar to that you have of tapeworms – the action is the same, the reaction is the same. It reminds you on a double level of the fear, both spiritual and physical, within you. It is not the actual creature itself, it is the contortion, the twisting that you dislike, and this is the fear you have to break. The constraint brought upon you in the physical level was done obliquely and left you almost in a position of helplessness for you were the victim of other people's manoeuvres.

The spiritual aspect you seek, the higher self knowledge filtering through to the lower self is hidden from conscious recognition surfacing sometimes when you least expect it. The snake works in a hidden way in deep grasses – and signifies the hidden part of you which you yet do not understand.

It is the 'not seeing' you mistrust, you like to be open and above board where all is seen and can then be dealt with. You are not able to deal with things which you cannot grasp and see clearly, and your rate of vibrational control at the moment does not enable you to do this. This is why you don't like the contortions of the hidden way, twisting out of your control and out of your understanding.

Doreen:–When I first started to meditate, Red Feather, I always appeared to be within the body going along its internal workings. Can you explain?

Red Feather:–The beginning of all things. To begin, the human being required cellular structure. When you first saw you saw through a cell to cellular structure, did you not? The body was unimportant what you had to see was within. You needed to see how the vibrations were drawn to each of the cells and how the cellular structure as a whole interacted and responded to the vibrations around it.

You saw colour when you began, this was a dual teaching process to begin the deep seeking into the beginnings of life expression; that you would begin to use colour to solve the beginnings when dealing with cellular structure – that is where you begin, that is where you have to learn, FROM THE BEGINNING YOU MUST LEARN THE BEGINNING, TO FIND THE BEGINNING.

You are beginning to learn about the use, result and purpose of colour. The essence of man is his spirit, the cellular structure the means to express that essence. You must see to understand how that colour essence plays a part in the individual soul life of the person who seeks. FROM THE BEGINNING LEARN THE BEGINNING TO FIND THE BEGINNING. Remember these words.

From the beginning you will find the reason for the end, to help man realise he is spirit first and foremost, his sojourn upon the earth simply a learning place in which to further his progression; that the decisions taken and life-style followed have a bearing upon his essence of spirit seen first of all in colour changes to the cellular structure and thence to physical illness within the body itself – imbalance between spirit essence and the expression of that essence in the life lived. You cannot start any subject in the depth you have chosen unless you go to that beginning of the beginning. Your teaching is to progress over the next few hundred years but you must in this physical life realise how intricate this work is to be – hence the Pandora's box, a little of which I have shown to you.

You are at the verge of the beginning of a very great and privileged understanding. You will never be upon your pathway in this life, the teaching is too vast; you are aiming for a time hence when mankind in general will not need drugs, will not need the supports of the material life-style which he has now. The training for this must begin many centuries beforehand. This then is the work you are about. You started this work a long time ago, you were then on the boundaries of it but circumstances did not permit further study – partly because the time was not right. Now the time is right to start learning for a future progression of mankind and the help you will be able to bring – again upon the earth.

Question 7

Anne:–Could Red Feather please explain a little more about the higher self. Is it part of us left behind on the higher plane. Is it our conscience, or is it you, who are higher in evolution, teaching us; or is it a part of the whole?

Red Feather:–The short answer is that the higher self is part of your own greater awareness, that awareness which is you. That awareness is part of all experiences which the you has ever experienced – that is the short answer.

It is a very deep understanding and is difficult for me to bring to you because it encompasses parts of teaching not yet given to you. I shall try to simplify but again as with some of the other questions, try to realise that there is a greater depth that you are as yet unable to plumb.

The higher self is made up of experiences gone before. Those experiences are dissected into the various qualities and quantities of that experience. Every experience that you have upon the earth at this time you feel, see, hear or do. Each of these actions has a reaction – each of those reactions has again sub-division into good and bad reactions, spiritual – non-spiritual, physical – non-physical, and so on down the line. The higher self takes from that experience the highest mean of experience for itself to add to itself, it does not take the lesser degrees because those have already been surpassed.

You add to the higher self experience by refinement of the lesser and gain a true rounded personality; the higher self can influence the lower self through those same true means. If, for instance, difficulty is experienced in life and the physical mind cannot find a solution the higher self responds and brings forward the strength and sometimes the clarity to help you through the crisis. I am sure you must have experienced this many times in the midst of a personal crisis when all experienced this many times in the midst of a personal crisis when all of a sudden the solution occurred from seemingly out of the blue.

The higher self brought that solution to you from a previous experience which you had. The higher self continually tries to influence your lower self towards a more spiritual attitude. In this way it takes to itself forces from around itself, from other spirit who perhaps have greater experience, greater understanding, and it tries to channel a little of that through to you. In this way it can so expand itself and the whole becomes more refined.

Anne:–I have not fully understood what you told me about the vibrational loop with which I will work. Could you please explain a little further?

Red Feather:–A little of the answer from the last question should supply a hint of information to you.

The link between the higher and lower selves is spiritual. Before mediumship can really be established there has to be a recognition that the physical self is working towards something definite and is spiritual. The self is a circle between the higher and lower degrees and can be influenced from the higher to the lower as the lower strives towards the higher – the loop. When this is established firmly and securely – there is the basis for mediumship, proper mediumship, spiritual mediumship.

You can have, what you term on earth, a psychic mediumship which does not really involve the higher self because it is to do with the material life, material aspirations, just occasionally branching out into the spiritual aspect. To have true spiritual mediumship with true teaching there must be the link between the higher and lower self within the mediumistic personality.

The higher self must have influenced the lower self towards a degree of spirituality which can be attained in a learning and a serving situation. When both the higher and the lower self are in harmony and agreement as to where the road will lead – that is the basis for future spiritual attainment.

Through this affinity between higher and lower degrees of the self there grows peace and harmony and with it a need to be of service to your fellow men. You want others to experience the happiness and the joyousness which comes from the fulfilment of such natural harmony.

This natural harmony then becomes a channel for mediumship; other helpers, guides, teachers are then able to come through this singular channel which has been established in spiritual love for the good and the benefit of all – including the self.

Due to its higher nature mediumship cannot be held by the physical mind alone and it must be given out that others can be touched by it. When a medium so developed reaches a certain stage there comes a point when they cannot hold that mediumship to themselves, it must have an outpouring of a spiritual nature – there can be no other result.

Anne:–Thank you. The other day you told me that I would work through the spiritual loop whilst the others used vibrations which went up/downwards. Is this because, in a way – a spiritual way, I am the infant of the group?

Red Feather:–No, you misunderstand my use of words. There is a difficulty when conveying spiritual aspects and using physical words, the physical words are not enough.

Let me try again. You have within you a particular strength which is able to relate equivocally to physical and spiritual matters. You see both clearly, the others of the group do not have the ability to separate then relate the two.

To someone who is searching spiritually for the very first time it seems the physical and spiritual are very closely interlinked though different; the physical needs, the physical wishes, the faint spiritual aspirations – they need someone to link the two, to show where the one can be tuned into the other; where the physical can be lessened and held yet strengthened toward the spiritual.

There will come a time when the spiritual will be stronger. As you know with yourself physical questions to do with a physical world in a physical situation do have spiritual intonations but always at the beginning of searching you ask in a physical aspect. You must have someone who is able to take the purely physical, explain the possible spiritual aspect, through this enhance the new physical understanding with a deeper spiritual insight.

This is your particular strength at this time, to relate one to the other, action with reaction to interaction. You are mediating between the physical and the spiritual, not between one idea and another, the idea is the same. You are not mediating in a state of war between ignorance and knowledge, you are mediating for greater understand of the real self. The lesser leading to the greater, back again to enhance the lesser in a new base of understanding and on towards the even greater. The loop of knowledge bridging and gaining progression for the real self.

Question 8

Anne:–Most circles seem to have a medium and a learning medium, the rest of the group giving power or receiving information. We appear to be a circle in which all are working to become mediumistic. We are taught solely by Spirit, which seems to surprise people. You have told us that there are many such circles working in a similar way to us. Is this then a new format being brought forward by Spirit?

Red Feather:–People should not be surprised. The reason you should attend a circle is for development of the higher self, through that comes mediumship for all.

It was perceived in the earlier times of circle development that power could only be generated for one person to develop mediumistically, this is not the standard set by Spirit; due to inadequate understanding of circle work it seemed to the members as if the power should be used to develop only one person, the others being latent developers. It is, therefore, custom we are against, this is what we have to change.

Many circles, like yours, are set up because there are not enough groups attached to the normal centres of development. In those circles the medium has greater sway over what happens and the development of that circle is formatted to what the controlling medium understands by development; happily in some circles the medium is willing to be led and taught herself by spirit as to the running of the circle. More circles like yours are set up because the members come to realise that through the development of the higher self comes mediumship. This should be the norm, everyone sits for higher development of the self – through that comes true mediumship. It does not work the other way around.

Anne:–Is this the reason that we were brought to this island for development so that we would not be able to be influenced by others?

Red Feather:–The affinity of harmony which established your base is the base to which you will always return. The harmony levels have built into them the environmental nature of your being upon your training ground. Therefore, when you refer to your base levels you naturally pick up harmonies which you have engendered in your basic training. Wherever you go – your island goes with you – it is your base. The harmonies of that island are an integral part of your future work. You have an abundance of nature on your doorstep, each strand of nature gives to you a certain strength which you will need. A strength of beauty, of naturalness, a strength of sound which is symphonic with nature. Within that balance you have a basis for your future work. Within that base your words, Anne, will have a naturalness which can be spoken so that everyone will understand; within that base, Doreen, your painting and your work will have the beauty and naturalness of nature. Within that same base Mary's healing work will have the gentleness of nature and the purity of true nature; within that base, Joy's work of mediumship at various levels will bring forth that same simplicity of the trueness of nature.

Those who are developing upon the earth do not realise the importance of the balance of nature in their training. This is why in some circles if sounds occur inharmonious to the person who is developing it hinders their development. If a person can be brought to a development level within their own environmental harmony the affinity has a greater chance of success.

Try to stress upon those who come to you and wish to develop that they must find their own level of harmony within their own natural (nature) surroundings for in that way they enhance the beauty which is theirs, the gentleness and the trueness of harmonic vibrations within themselves. Remember that Spirit is a balance between nature and God – essentially Spirit and if all or part of that balance is missing there cannot be complete harmony.

You yourselves have an abundance of nature upon your doorstep. You have the harmony and motion of the sea – the vibrational waves, you have wind – although I often hear you wish that it had less prominence – it brings to you the central drive and velocity which you need for your work. There are the bays and the dunes, the peacefulness of the green grass, the expanse of open sky, those are the strengths which are particular to you.

You are all much more complex characters than you realise. Nature plays a greater part in your development and aspirations than you know. If more circles could realise that this is where their basic strength lies then perhaps they could be structured differently.

Always upon the earth there is a push to develop, the push to run before you can walk, the push to run before you can even begin to understand. Circle teaching must be brought to a more inspirational level; a level in which the higher self is allowed to express itself on the material plane. What is needed is to understand that the development of self, rather than just mediumistic development, is why true mediumship occurs – then you have the beginning of an understanding which can bring benefit to all who wish to sit. The structure must be changed, there must be a new understanding, there must be a reorganisation of priorities to give the higher self its real priority. In that way all circles will become mediumistic, spiritually mediumistic – it cannot fail.

Anne:–This house in which we sit, particularly this room, is impregnated with spirit. Will this be lost when we leave, or will you be able to utilise it in some other way?

Red Feather:–Nothing is ever lost. All vibrations gained are kept – and in a sense hoarded – by the place in which they are gained. They are only picked up by those who are sensitive enough to realise what they are. It may not be the next incomers to your house, or the ones after that, but at some point in the life of this house they will be picked up by those who can best enjoy. It is in a sense, similar to healing vibrations, when dealing with a patient healing rays are put into them which come from God, which are needed, which are good. Those healing rays are stored within the body, released and used by the body when it needs them at the rate in which it needs them. So it is with your home.

Anne asks which elements are important to each of us.

Red Feather:–Doreen – For greater balance you need trees around you but you can make up for this lack with flowers; there will come a time in your development when more refinement is needed, then trees will be presented to you and enhance you even further.

Mary – You get benefit more from the earth, from this you get the base roots and know if the content of the soil is right and what will grow in it to best advantage. This is a judging of balance between the seed sown and the soil into which it is to be sown, representing the balance between the spiritual and the physical as required in the healing.

Joy – You hold a great variety of strengths given from all the vibrations of the sea and air. From the depth and motion of the sea is drawn strength from its various depths, also from the vibrations of the air is received inspiration and freedom to search in thought. This is why you feel city life so restricting – being cut off from the base needs of the spiritual self.

For Anne – These are as with Joy, water and air, but with you air comes first. You draw inspiration from the air, this is why you enjoy walking with nothing upon your head going face into the wind and meeting the element head-on taking in its full driving force or gentle waft as given to you. The water is a pool with a whirling central core boring right down into it – the edges becoming tender little ripples, this shows your liking to get to the very centre of any thought or teaching in order to understand it more clearly without fudge. This gained information is then spread out in little ripple-like vibrations to reach the corners of the mind leading it towards an even deeper knowledge.

Question 9

Anne:–Jesus was a manifestation of the Christ consciousness, what then is the relationship of the Christ to God?

Red Feather:–Christ in relationship to God is the manifestation of that degree of understanding acceptable to those who receive. God is infinite, in a world such as yours there has to something which can be touched and related to spiritually. As your minds cannot achieve this infinite distinction there is a manifestation of God – in this instance known as Christ. There are other manifestations of the same given different names.

In your world the Christ consciousness is the part of God which is able to be related to by those upon the earth and by those who need this continuous understanding when they pass over into spirit. It is the acceptable face of God to those who seek Him and to each it brings that degree of understanding acceptable at that time to draw them forward and progress. The Christ consciousness is always a step ahead of your own understanding inviting you to explore more deeply the truth of spirit.

Anne:–Is it levels within God?

Red Feather:–It is levels within God, but it is always mainly relating man to his God. God cannot be touched by man in any other understandable way in his present degree of progression.

Anne:–Have we gone through all forms of life during our evolution, i.e. vegetable, mineral, animal?

Red Feather:–Man has always been man. Spirit has always been spirit, but that spirit is able to encompass within it all that can be experienced by life forms. This may seem a contradiction to you. Man has evolved from the spirit of God, within that he has a higher understanding, within that higher understanding he can take to himself experiences of other forms.

He can understand that experience without actually going through it – by his spirit touching that of the flower or the animal he can take from it what he needs to know. It is essentially a question of spirit touching spirit – that is the way the experience is gained, not physical man becoming another form of life.

Once again you have entered upon a deep area, one for which your teaching has not fully prepared you. I find difficulty in bringing examples to you because of the limited understanding, but I shall try.

A flower is first a seed, a bulb, stem, and leaves before a flower, then it grows receiving its nourishment from the earth, the air, the elements. Man is a seed of Spirit, evolves into greater understanding of the bulb, not yet formed into anything but the spirit evolving; it then gathers to it experiences which nourish it – helping it to grow and expand. From that comes the beginning of growth into shape – as the bulb into the stem and leaves. Thus man evolves into something more – into man himself – a human being, the limbs are there, the body is there, but full understanding is not.

The flower blooms, it reaches its peak of perfection, then once more dies away down the stem, back into the bulb, back into the earth to re-seed again another year. Man lives, gathers his experiences, he dies returning to spirit as spirit – an enlarged spirit; he can then re-seed once more as man once more to gain wider experience, to live once more, die once more and continue. The daffodil is always a daffodil, man always man. It is the experience which differs, you bloom and grow by the quality of your seed. The more a flower's seed is refined, the more it is helped by receiving better nourishment – the better the flower, so it is with man, he re-seeds out of his own experience, out of his own learning, to become better spirit, to re-seed to become better man to better spirit.

Man has much to learn, the spirit is something which longs for growth but not always does it receive the nourishment it requires. As with a flower you can have bad growth, distorted growth – likewise within the spirit of a man and perhaps his lifetime purpose is lost through this for he has distorted the spirit self by using his life experience in a wrong way.

Rather than becoming a distorted spirit he becomes a delayed spirit, he needs to re-graft to the original spirit stem which nourished him and in that way he re-grows, this time with understanding. Man takes to himself that which he needs for his growth and it is his responsibility to grow spiritually through earthly experience the way he should. The flower must grow in the way of its seed, it has no direction over how or where it will grow – it must grow where it is planted.

Man has greater freedom than that, he can choose his experience, he can choose whether to learn from that experience or whether to disregard it. In this way is man greater than the spirit of the flower, or the bird, or the animal. He is none the less of God than they and is as precious to God as they, but he has a measure for his own progression which is his responsibility.

In this way, too, the spirit of man refines itself. Flowers are refined by spirit for God by others, not so man; we in spirit can help, we can guide, we can tutor, but we cannot live for you. We can give you the nourishment, help you with the growth and encouragement by gently reminding you of your duties towards your own spirit – but we cannot take over these duties. Your growth is YOUR RESPONSIBILITY for your spirit. Your responsibility is of God.

Mary:–How can I become a better channel to aid this new form of (soul) healing?

Red Feather:–Your subject is so complex and the concept so new to your group that none of you have knowledge of it.

The above question has been answered many times. There is nothing you have to do other than that you do. Follow your own intuition, you will never go wrong, perception will increase. You have put in two years of solid work building up and trusting that feeling of vibration between yourself and Silver Dove, now you respond instantly to what he requires of you. You may not always understand – but the instant spiritual response to what you feel is all that is required of you meantime.

The answer to your question is always the same for there is no other advice of any use to give – Respond to the self within, respond more quickly, more accurately and the soul will mirror the need.

Question 10

Anne:–There are many segments, facets of the whole spirit, each giving forth expressions in a variety of ways and in a variety of different places. Would I be right in thinking that this again has to do with affinity, in that each is an expression of the same whole?

Red Feather:–Yes.

Anne:–Am I also right in the assumption that spirit and consciousness are the same. That consciousness is a part of spirit, or indeed, is spirit itself?

Red Feather:–Consciousness is the expression of spirit.

Anne:–Some time ago you told me that Spirit was pure but required to be tried and tested. I have still not understood how Spirit that is pure is able to express itself in wrong-doing. If this does not come from Spirit, how does it come into being – what within us is impure?

Red Feather:–As you have consciousness in a positive (knowledgeable) sense so you have facets of consciousness in a negative (ignorant) sense, two halves of the same whole – action and reaction. As each affinity has a positive well-being affect upon the Spirit there is also a negative side which must become positive through experience to lift the recognised consciousness to a higher level, to give birth to the next level of consciousness which needs to be accepted. Ignorance becomes knowledge thereby exposing further knowledge yet to be gained. Through action you have a positive polarity with knowledge. Reaction is the opposite but also the same in that action is the cause with reaction its effect; there is never only action, reaction, action, reaction – rather the chain is – action reaction becoming action to reaction and so on.

The greater always pulls up the lesser; the more positive knowledge pulls up the negative ignorance to change that negative into positive polarity thus creating in turn another negative waiting its turn for positive action.

Within the facets of your diamond each has its action and reaction, the facet is enhanced when the action causes the reaction to become action itself. The whole level of the facet is then lifted and cleared towards positivity.

Consciousness acts as this clearing for Spirit in that each experience contains the different degrees of positive and negative and also contains the durability of the Spirit within. Each facet contains the process to change the negative into positive. As you experience life and its lessons you take the strength from the positive effects of your actions to enlighten the negative, learning as you progress through life which action leads to a good reaction and furthers your understanding of life; but if you have taken the wrong understanding from the given lesson and dealt with it in the wrong way the reaction remains reaction through its ignorance and negative polarity, further gain being denied until ignorance becomes knowledge.

Anne:–Is it similar to the law of retribution?

Red Feather:–In a sense, but it is much more deeply aligned to the spirit than is given credit. People do not realise how they can change things for the good of themselves, to raise their limits by changing the negative reactions into positive action through right thinking followed by right action. The facets are ever changing as you progress; the degrees of positivity and negativity held within your being determine the extent of knowledge gained from ignorance. Consciousness is the thread along which you travel to do this. This is why you feel some things are right and some things are wrong, consciousness and its link to the physical mind through conscience is your guiding light.

Anne:–Please explain further about action and reaction, can you better clarify, I still do not yet realise the cause of evil.

Red Feather:–Action and reaction, positive and negative, good and bad, all degrees of knowledge and ignorance.

Right action acted upon in a positive manner will always result in progressive knowledge; wrong action acted upon in a negative fashion will result in continued ignorance and a repeat of that reaction until at last it dawns upon the individual that there must be another way of bringing about change in his life. Until that happens he will commit the same degree of ignorance over and over again bringing with it the negative effects of such action – evil being a degree of that negativity.

Anne:–So someone could do a bad action – abhor that which they had done, bringing from it a good new action, or do a similar bad action not seeing it as bad, therefore becoming through its repetition a criminal.

Red Feather:–Yes.

Anne:–You still have not answered the main part of my question. Where does evil come from, which part of us brings this into being?

Red Feather:–The answer lies in the degree of ignorance within every progressing soul. The question is very complex and there are other matters which affect the answer which I will not advance at this time.

Given the complexity of the question I have this to say – Spiritual man is as God designed and desired man to be. Mankind is as man has made him. The difference between the two is the progressive rate of the soul from the one extreme to the other. All perfection is held within Spiritual being, all defectiveness is held within mankind – defective spirit, but spirit which can be righted, which can be drawn back to the original purity, greatly strengthened by the experiences.

It has to be a gradual progress of learning, of eliminating the defective parts of man's thinking because it is not merely man's action which is defective, it is man's thought. Thought always comes before action, no matter how instant the action it has to be thought of first. It is man's thought that is defective, that which must be righted.

The channel which the spiritual self conducts to the physical self to let you know whether you are proceeding along the right or wrong way is called conscience. It is a link which can be transcended by the spirit self and by the advisers in the spirit world. The more highly attuned your consciousness is to the God feeling of your higher self the greater influence that God feeling can have on your physical life through the conscience link.

There are some in your world who deny the existence of God, who deny the existence of their higher self and the cause of good in the world – they have closed the door to that positive link preferring instead the materialistic and the short-term advantage as they see it. They have, in effect, no working positive conscience, only a negative and self-ignorant viewpoint of their own immediate needs on a delusory scale.

This is what gives you degrees of ignorance, some of which contain the low degree described as "evil". There is no brake upon evil intent, evil thoughts, nothing to make them draw back. The spirit self cannot reach the physical mind to apply the conscience factor to hold back from evil action.

One of the greatest stumbling-blocks we have from spirit in your world is this lack of conscience connection between the spirit higher self and the physical life being lived. If that link could be strengthened there would be a great deal less sadness in your world. There would be more brightness, more happiness, because people would respond to the higher being which is themselves. The lower always responds to the higher; the higher is stronger, its intent purer, therefore it overcomes the weakness. The lack of conscience working between the physical and the spirit debars this effect and man's thinking has full rein, it can go in the direction it wants to go regardless of anything else, for all have freewill and that freewill is sacrosanct.

If such a man closes the door upon spirit and is intent upon doing evil there is very little we can do to change his course. We must await him opening that door just a little to let a tiny ripple of his own higher self come through, attach itself, and so re-establish the link of spirit to the lower self. This then is what you call evil.

Anne:–Thank you, that has made it much clearer, I will think on it again.

Anne:–May I now come to reincarnation, Is it right that each facet of

the whole, rather of an affinity, has to incarnate into each sphere of
experience but only once. That the many incarnations – say to earth –
are in fact different facets, but each coming only once?

Red Feather:–Each facet of spirit will reincarnate as often as it is
needed, where it is needed, to gain in knowledge. You cannot progress
to another lesson until you have fully learned the one being given.
Included in that are all its facets for the limit of understanding which
that soul at that time has achieved. Therefore, if that soul progresses
well during the one incarnation and has learnt all its lessons to that
degree of understanding, another level has been attained and another
incarnation can be given with the same situations, but at a higher
degree level requiring a deeper insight and responsibility.

Anne:–From the line of affinity, can only one person incarnate at a
time into any one place?

Red Feather:–Not necessarily. As each spirit is different, so each spirit's
requirements are different. Therefore if the requirements are there for
more than one part of the affinity, then any number can surface.

Anne:–Is the amount of spirit contained in each creation static? Is it
the consciousness which changes, increasing its ability of expression
through evolution?

Red Feather:–The availability for perfect spirit expression is there for
everyone. It is the degree of enlightenment which controls the
evolution of spirit. Spirit is constant, Spirit is pure, Spirit is full
enlightenment.
    The degree of enlightenment granted to each incarnating spirit varies
with the experience it requires. By this I mean – a single spirit
travelling upon its road of evolution requires different experiences to
gather strength unto itself. Each strength requires a varying degree of
spiritual enlightenment to help it along its way. As experiences are
progressed through and accepted into the spirit self gaining spiritual
security, so the degree of enlightenment granted to that spirit is
heightened.
    The world must come to realise that man matters, that man is
responsible, and that the world can only become a better place as man

accepts his own responsibility. To do that he must first be made aware of that responsibility. First of all we must make man think, then he must act towards his own responsibility.

Question 11

Anne:–Can you please explain to us how control is established?

Red Feather:–It is your old friend the affinity line. I will use the affinity line between Joy and myself as an example, though there are variations for others pairs and other groups.

Anne:–Please explain, Red Feather.

Red Feather:–There are degrees of affinity and within any single affinity line there are degrees of attainment. The main affinity is very broadly based and encompasses the many degrees required by a developing soul as it strives to gain knowledge and purification.

This degree of affinity had been developed through other levels in the past, gradually I have built up sensitivity to reach this present level and in time this will build to something greater yet to come.

In the beginning the affinity line is established through the original affinity of SPIRIT LIKE, but a spark of mutual like, spirit like attracting like. I noticed within this embryo affinity that spark which could be sensitised.

Those higher had directed my thoughts towards this, had explained to me what could be done with this embryo spark if I would be willing to put in many, many years of work to bring that spark to be a light, to a serviceable understanding. This was built upon.

To do this I had to give this 'like spark' thought that it needed to train itself in this affinity – to give it an attraction if you like; it had to be deeply implanted so that in the physical being the soul would still unite and carry that embryo spirit into greater production of thought and duty.

The soul has to be willing to do this, I could not impose my will upon her soul, that would be a limitation of her freedom – and that is not allowed. I had to work through her expression of freedom to gain

her confidence, to help her choose that line for herself in her own time.
We built upon this affinity very slowly because the work which has to be done is of such a serious and deep nature with far reaching effects upon other people. There had to be complete confidence built up between the two of us and this has been done over many, many years. Very gradually have I guided, always there, unknown for a large amount of the time – just there.

She now works easily with me, responds easily to me, above all – she trusts me. To get that trust I have guided her soul thoughts into her physical mind to enable her physical mind gain acceptance without complete understanding. She bends her will to mine, as I bend my will to those higher than myself, all in God's love and service; a bending of the will towards – so therefore is control established. It is a control established and worked *within her own free will* – that is what is important.

You need people for this kind of work who are not afraid to say what they believe if they truly believe it. This can sometimes bring problems before control has been fully established because the physical mind can reject. In this instance it was accepted – not without question, but accepted rationally, deeply thought about, deeply researched, and then fully accepted.

We do not use our affinity attractions in a way which will overbear, we cannot do that, we work through love and free will; if we can gain those two things then love of God is established, and that is the control we use.

The control through love has no bounds, no limits, is not of my volition nor of hers – it is God's – therefore it is not control as you understand it, it is a walk hand in hand in God's service, both of us playing our part to bring to those who listen, those who come to seek, a little of the truth we have been privileged to share.

I dislike the use of the word "control", it brings to the physical mind the thought that the medium has no free will of her own, that she has no worthy thought of her own, that she is completely within my power – and this I reject. She is an individual in her own right, she is strong-minded in her own right, but she has – in all of that – a deep love of God and His work, she also has a *soul need* to do this work and that is her control. Thus the control comes from within herself as my control comes from within myself, between these two is the degree of affinity for this work.

Anne:–Does the affinity line have to do with the various degrees of colour, e.g. the gold line of affinity, the blue line of affinity, and so on?

Red Feather:–You are talking not about the broader based affinity line but the degrees of attainment within the broad base. You are aware that in the spirit world there are notes of harmony, colours of harmony; if the two are combined together on the correct vibrational level as they rise in refinement they become an affinity.

Within the degree of the broad affinity line there are various avenues for you to tread; on the golden road you are seeking knowledge. For the moment you are working your way through the vibrational range of the golden road as it is not in complete harmony with the colour and the note of music; you are all a little off colour, off key because you are still learning, still searching for the rudiments of spiritual truth.

In time that road will diversify, within the golden road there are many shades, you will find your own key, your own note within one of those shades and you can transfer from the lighter to the deeper to the more ethereal as you progress.

Anne:–Always on the yellow?

Red Feather:–For the moment, yes, but not necessary always. Your friend Mary works on the blue road of healing and her degree of required wisdom is contained within her own colour vibration. There are different roads for different facets of your training. At the moment your need is for wisdom and so you are on the golden road.

Question 12

Anne:–Does the heart have a greater role than just the physical function?

Red Feather:–The heart is the seat of the emotional centre. It is the connection between the emotional spirit and the physical emotion established. It is the link between the thought forms and actual experience. It is the centre through which the God feeling works, the gathering together centre of conscience, the centre where are pooled together the links between the physical and the spiritual, where the physical ascends to the spiritual, where the spiritual influences the physical.

The heart centre as opposed to the heart organ – which, I believe, is what you mean – is one to which not enough attention is paid. It is the one which picks up perception, feeling within you, gives voice to your spirit self when there is neither hearing nor seeing. It is the bridging point for the spiritual values to come into physical life.

This centre enhances physical life, is responsible for the way in which physical life is lived. Any constriction upon the gradual spiritual expansion of the heart centre shows itself in many ways; through poor physical health, in poor appreciation of spiritual values, in attitudes towards known and unknown subjects.

The heart centre helps the physical mind open itself through the emotions to greater thoughts and actions of a compassionate nature. It is your gateway to both the spiritual and the physical kingdom of well-being.

Doreen:–In a lesson some time ago to me you stated – "in the future mankind in general will no longer require drugs, nor would he need the support of the material life-style which he has now". What does this embrace?

Red Feather:–The time is very far hence. A time to come when the fulfilment of soul healing as beginning to be learnt by the little one of Silver Dove will by then be common practice. I am speaking of a time when colour and music will be fully understood, when man himself will work in harmony with nature.

The need for drugs has come about because man does not understand nature, colour or music. Through man's own being he has brought about a position where he cannot use the forces of nature, he cannot use his own intellect as given by God due to the need for spiritual realignment.

When soul healing is in common practice man will not need drugs as he will be able to use from within his own spirit self the necessary qualities which nature has in abundance. He will be able to balance them, use the colours and properties of nature – all properties of nature – for there are some as yet undiscovered, not undiscovered in substance but in meaning. Man has to travel a long way for this to happen.

When man seeks to harmonise instead of control nature then he will no longer need drugs for he will understand the fulfilment of nature – the part which nature has to play in his own well-being. That is the time of which I spoke.

Anne:–Reading from The Betty Book it states in the 'do it now' Chapter:–"That there are in this very earth life certain faculties for beginning our spiritual quest that are lacking in the next state of existence." Can you provide us with more detailed information as to why?

Red Feather asks Anne to rephrase her question.

Anne:–It seems that when we are upon the earth plane this is the best time to open ourselves to spirit because when we go back to spirit there are not the same facilities there and so it will be harder and longer for us.

Red Feather is disagreeing.

Anne says:–If we have not opened ourselves and become aware of spirit, it appears to be much harder for us from the spirit end.

Red Feather:–You are never unaware of spirit. You may think you are, but no one has ever been unaware of spirit. As you ARE spirit and aware of yourself, you CANNOT be unaware of spirit. You may be unaware of what spirit is.

Because you have never been unaware of spirit you do not need to reopen yourself to spirit, what you have to do is unlock the key of understanding spirit. If you rephrase the question to ask about the reawakening of the understanding of spirit – then I can accept your question.

Red Feather shows Joy a picture of a tree – a fully-grown tree. He is showing the very first thought cell of the seed of that tree. That thought cell of that seed is always there – like your always spirit, but the cell of that seed cannot realise the full potential of that tree as it is still a cell, it has to grow a little. With each part of that growth each cell gathering to itself another cell, its expansion and its understanding of itself grows. In this way a seed is then formed with the full potential of the tree, full potential of spirit growth in its own time and in its own fruition but still not realised nor recognised by the cells gathering together of that seed.

Sometimes that seed is stunted, sometimes that seed is over-nourished – therefore good is washed or burnt out, only when there is proper growth does that seed come to its own potential and next stage of growth.

Anne:–That still does not explain why it is easier to do upon the earth rather than we return to spirit.

Red Feather shows Joy arid land and very good land. He is showing the cells of the seed being planted in both. He shows that in the fertile ground those seeds come together very quickly, in the arid land they still exist but growth is stunted.

Red Feather continues:–The cells of your own seed, sapling, or your half-grown tree, will be transplanted to where there is fertile ground of experience for you whether that be on earth or another sphere initially.

God gives you experience where you can best grow but it is up to you to help that growth by living correctly and according to your soul need. If you disregard the needs of your soul and do not want to recognise spirit thinking you are physically greater than the spirit within, every experience will show its negative side, thus the land which was fertile becomes arid and spiritual growth is unbalanced. It is what you do with the opportunity for growth which unlocks your potential. There is potential within all realms however that expression is perceived, other worlds or the earth, growth of spirit will occur given suitable opportunity and I have to break through this 'earth understanding' barrier to help you realise that you are far more complex beings than you realise. The earth CANNOT give you all the experiences you need for growth, it CAN give you valuable lessons in a multiplicity of ways helpful to spiritual growth.

Anne:–From the beginning of my training I have been mostly aware of just four colours – purple, red, green and gold. I have not been fully satisfied by answers I have received as to why. The other morning it suddenly came to me that these colours represented the loop spoken of by you. Have I understood correctly? If so, are the colours seen by each of us during meditation of more significance than we have as yet realised?

Red Feather:–You will not be satisfied by this answer either. We have always told you that there is more to colour than you realise. Colour has great importance; it has within your own circle a very great importance, you must use colour constructively by interpreting the meaning and its use.

The reason you will not be satisfied with my answer is because it is much deeper than you have stated. As you reach stages in your own spiritual journey you will come to recognise what each stage of colour means in its correct context. You are beginning to work on the first colour.

Anne:–I looked at the four colours – purple – the spiritual side of the loop, red – the physical side of the loop, with the gold of wisdom bringing forth harmony (green) to all.

Red Feather:–You have sections within you lives which are colour orientated to the one particular pathway for your expansion at this time.

At the moment you are going through your red phase – the understanding of physical life and its values, the re-establishment of the same, the replanting of the same and until you have finished the phase you cannot go on to the next. All your thoughts kicking and bucking, throwing out and taking in – the physical mind realignment to the spiritual self influence. There is an even deeper implication to what has just been said but your understanding must grow a little more before it can be brought forward.

When you have come to realisation, accepted and harmonised the new understanding of yourself and your surroundings you go to the next phase – a step higher and deeper. We each have our own colour strength at any one particular spiritual stage of our lives. Mary's predominating colour is blue, Doreen's colour is green. Joy is going through two colours, going from the red into the yellow – not yet finished with the red, though allowing more yellow to enter.

Anne:–Many problems within the earth plane arise from our different cultures and skin tones. I have wondered if we have not all at some stage in our evolution been of a different culture and skin tone, which would then make farcical the lack of understanding which exists on all sides.

Red Feather:–There is a two-fold reason for this. Partly the differing skin tones are to do with nature and the habitats in which you live upon the earth. That is purely a physical reason but there is a deeper reason. Man's disharmony is very great. He finds it difficult to relate to things which are different from his own being. He does not think nor understand deeply enough. He thinks that because a man's culture, colour is different from his own, that man must therefore be inferior. Until mankind realises that ALL SPIRITS ARE ONE WITHIN GOD THE FATHER there cannot be harmony within himself.

Aside from the natural physical habitat this deeper reason for different cultures and skin tones is to try to bring about a deeper understanding of values which are similar though shown in different ways. It is a simple way, an obvious way, in which God chooses to bring forth harmony in mankind; to help all see that ALL are God's children. The physical eyes do not see clearly enough, the physical reasoning is not deep enough, physical thought on different cultures is insufficient in scope.

Man must come to realise that he must go deeply within himself to find the similar strain of nature that runs through all mankind. Until he can contain this simple idea as proven upon your earth, he is not yet ready for man's greater spiritual lessons ahead.

Anne:–I thank Red Feather for his answer which I can see to be very good. I did ask in previous lives we had been of different cultures and skin tones, because if so, surely we cannot condemn what we ourselves were in previous times.

Red Feather:–The spirit within should be able to recognise all cultures are one. The being of a different culture and colour in a different lifetime cannot add one iota to that original idea. You have to realise it from where you are.

It can happen that people come back into different religions, different parts of the world with different skin tones, that is not the prime thing they have to experience. It is the experience itself which is brought to them – regardless of skin colour – which they need and can only perhaps be given in a certain part of the world. You would not get the same experiences here as those people in the third world, would you, therefore it is the experience which is paramount not the colour of the skin. Brotherhood is the same wherever you are and you should be able to realise that whatever past experiences you have gone through.

Anne:–I had thought that if one could say – in your last life you yourself where brown or black, how then can you condemn?

Red Feather:–It would carry no further weight if they do not have that within them already to realise it. It is the depth of a question people must probe for themselves, they must then realise that all men are one. I take your point, it is a good one, it lends itself to greater depth than you anticipated.

Question 13

During our tea-break Anne commented on the many times we must have been carnate before, and what a pity it was that we had lost that already learned – in that we could not remember.

Red Feather came through with the following:–I wish to correct misinterpretation. You have not lost what you had before, all that you had gained you still carry but all that you have gained is not necessary to this lifetime – therefore it awaits. All that you have gained, you regain during your sleep period – you never lose it, you cannot lose a gain. But what you have to relearn is a physical mind acceptance of spirit gain.

Anne:–This is a degree again?

Red Feather:–It is. You are here this lifetime to open and reopen a facet of your own self for further development to give a greater refinement to your own whole. If you did not do this you would not expand your spirit self. The experiences you are being given and are now having difficulty with in this present life are facets of yourself needed for future work and this is the time for fruition.

You had before you came a lesser understanding of those same truths you now accept but you require an extension of that knowledge – from knowledge into practical use. You learn the theory in spirit life then you come to put it into practise – this is your classroom. All you have to do is open that link to the knowledge you already have and put it into being.

This is why I stated earlier that you yourselves gained and grew, spirit always was, always is. You know the knowledge already, now you must make it grow.

Doreen:–Could you please tell us – is it coincidental that the colour rays we are following at the moment, those given to us by you the other night, seem to have a connection with the planetary signs we were born under, i.e. Anne – red, early Leo. Joy – leaving red entering yellow, later Leo. Doreen – green, Virgo. Mary – blue, Pisces.

Red Feather:–Nothing in your life is by accident, all is by design from the Creator. What you have in the colours so determined by those birth signs is the level of understanding you have attained plus the level of attainment which you can proceed towards. All is contained within your colours, within your birth sign, but that is only a little part of what must be considered. It is a little part of the whole. You have in your birth sign a directive force given to enable you to carry out the attainment level for the future. You have within your birth sign the level of understanding which you have gained and keep for that facet of your development now taking place.

You each have many facets, many lifetimes. Each is a progression. Each birth date and time with circumstances respect give to you the exact circumstances for full attainment levels for that facet of your personality and soul growth which is needed at this particular time. There are latent qualities within each of you still to be developed, those cannot be delivered to attainment levels under your present circumstances – they await in abeyance.

The colours within your group have great significance. Look at the four colours, look at how they balance each other and provide a ladder to greater understanding within the group as a whole. Anne is rooted in the red of physical life – her task to understand how spirit works through physical life and gains its freedom into the higher love of universal brotherhood, all working together as one for the greater love of God.

The next step on the ladder is taken up by Joy who carries this deeper into bringing forward the knowledge of spirit (yellow) into a working understanding within physical life (red).

Doreen then takes the following step of integrating that knowledge and bringing it into harmony (green) within the physical mind allowing it to provide the bridge over into the deeper meanings of spiritual insight and values.

Mary brings her healing (blue) compassion to bear upon all of this work. She is the channel for healing the physical ailments and more importantly – healing the soul itself. The blue of seeking a clearer way ahead through healing, harmony and love; teaching the soul as it progresses along its chosen pathway.

Doreen:–Do we progress through all of the colours from red to purple?

Red Feather:–You must keep in mind that you cannot develop one facet of you personality further than the others can reach. You must always keep in mind the development of the whole; one colour will never be allowed to move so far forward that the others cannot attain harmony. Therefore, in a sense, all colours are contained until the whole is able to move forward into new vibrational levels.

When a colour is in ascendance it denotes the strongest lesson you are learning at that particular time, but you are not confined to that one colour for as it is extended into understanding there are lesser lessons within that experience to bring forward all other colours to keep them within reach, within bounds. You must develop as a whole within balance.

Sometimes a combination of colours are developed together if different strengths are needed to take you through a certain life experience. If, for instance, you need a great deal of courage to get through an illness but you need gentleness and compassion to appreciate what others are doing for you – those two strengths, having different colours, would be developed together. In the same way – should you need a different brand of courage, as in bravery in a war situation – you also need the compassion for your enemies. Therefore, no one colour can be set against another – they must harmonise, otherwise there is incomplete development.

Anne:–As spirit energy, are we in reality – light? If so, white light, i.e. God contains all colours which we have to progress through. Is each colour, therefore, a facet of the God force?

Red Feather:–Yes.

Anne:–In Joy's progression I note that she moves out of the red into the yellow. Is this because the red and yellow combination bring forth the orange, so that by the development of the red and the yellow, development of the orange will also take place?

Red Feather:–In Joy's development I used the orange to drive. I get it from the red – the physical life force and from the yellow – knowledge of her spirit being. The combination of her need to know and understand her spirit and its purpose gives her the drive found within the orange. It propels her forward to reach the deeper levels within.

Physical life (red) was felt not to contain all to satisfy the unknown need which spurred (orange) her forward. She explored various avenues looking to satisfy this need but only when she began to look within the self for the answers (yellow) did she bring the spark of her spirit to bear upon her physical understanding of life. This knowledge drew her interest deeper towards the meaning of her life and brought her to a balance of harmony (green) and a measure of peace to the unknown need.

From this new base of understanding she began to search more deeply into spirit values (blue), in its turn this brought them more in touch with her own spirit being and she began to 'see, hear and be intuitively guided of spirit' (indigo) opening the way to the higher guidance found within the violet.

Question 14

Anne:–Is perpetuation carried out in similar fashion to that of amoeba, but of light many times over, and is perpetuation of spirit still continuing today? If so, will it be an ongoing procedure throughout eternity?

Red Feather:–The short answer is yes, but again it holds degrees of perpetuation. Only that which is ongoing and positive will perpetuate. In any one strain of perpetuation, no matter what is being perpetuated, there is good and bad strains within. The good will always strengthen and survive, the lesser – I don't want to say bad – serves its purpose in this way; the lesser holds perpetuation as long as it is valuable to that perpetuation. By that I mean, it has a time span attached to it, it serves a purpose for a certain length of time to give strength to that which is good or to make more acceptable that which is wholly good.

Perpetuation is twofold – not good and bad but greater and lesser. The greater always contains the lesser but the lesser cannot contain the greater, therefore, when the greater has outgrown the lesser, the lesser will subside.

Let me explain further:–A weakness is permitted within a strain of perpetuation if in the long run it gives strength to the strength. You, as such, are not fully developed spirit, none of us are, because there is no end to perpetuation – not as we understand it. Within each of us there are greater and lesser strains running side by side as we have not the attainment of take complete purity within complete perpetuation – it has to be done in stages. Stages are gone through with the help of the lesser strain but always purifying to leave behind that which is outgrown.

How can I more easily explain this to you? Let us take wine, fermenting wine: to begin with are all the necessary ingredients required to make that wine. You have a period when the wine grows to fermentation, then there is a period of stillness and the wine purifies, but the action of the fermentation has taken away the impurities and caused them to become pure. This is what happens with the greater and lesser in perpetuation. It brings purity to that which was an amalgam of impurity.

Anne:–The other day I was asked by Mrs M. how she could carry out self-healing between our visits to ease her pain. Would you be kind enough to tell us how this should have been answered?

Red Feather:–The only necessary thing this lady requires to do is to take the peace and the stillness of God into her thoughts and thence to her physical being. In this way she enlarges her own spirit within. This opens the way for those who love her in spirit to come closer to her, to give her greater strength to get through the infirmities of old age.

Self-healing is a process of acceptance of yourself as you are within physical limitations, but bringing to that your spiritual self and strength to help you over the difficulties. Your physical body brings its own encumbrances, you cannot escape them while expressing life on earth.

Anne:–Could you please explain the difference, if any, between the group soul and the affinity line?

Red Feather:–I will endeavour to condense for you. Imagine yourself as a spirit whole – just you yourself, you then meet with a like-minded soul and there are then two of you. The two expand each other, share the same feelings and vibration rate, the experiences of the two are greater than that of the one – a group spirit of only two people.

There is no definite setting for a group soul, no end to numbers as such. It is like this – you take a pebble in your hand and you throw it into a still lake, that pebble causes ripples through to the shore, each of those ripples represents a group soul. Each one acts, interacts and reacts to all others. As a group soul expands – like that thrown pebble – it can reach further and further outwards, its experiences become greater and greater, it can have wider and wider effects for good but it never loses its central motion from the beginning. God causes this centre, this movement in each of us separately and collectively.

Like-minded souls are the one multiplied in expansion, experience and love by each other for each other, there is no end. There is no difference between the group soul and the affinity line. If you are in a group soul you are attracted by like-minded souls, therefore, you must have a similar affinity. Let me go further:–The greatest amount of good can be done by like-minded souls, like feeling souls, who have the same interest in spirit, the same rate of expansion, the same willingness to group together to gain the expansion for them all.

As the individual soul expands it longs for greater experience and as it seeks its perfection in the making it will develop positive interests in one way or another, and will then generate towards others of like purpose to create the experience and expansion which that soul has reached and needs at that time.

As that expansion moves and works increasing the rate individually as well as for the whole group all move gradually onwards to the next stage of the affinity line.

Anne:–Thank you. May I further ask, we are four here in circle, are we all on the same affinity line?

Red Feather:–Not necessarily. You have reached this point in your understanding where your affinity line requires experience to be worked to expand. You choose to come back unto earth to get that expansion. If you can come to realise that your reason for being here is to expand yourselves as individuals and your affinity group as a whole, then you will come to realise what I am talking about. You are here to gain positive experience of theory already learnt. You are putting that learning into practice in physical life so that when you return to spirit you will be that much better, that much more expanded. You will be further along your affinity line ready for the next stage of lessons to which you have progressed.

It is an experience you all need at this time, you are like-minded but you need application to expand your spirit soul in the way required. This question is allied to the one of perpetuation, the two are the same. You are perpetuating within yourselves your soul need, your soul purpose – you could not do it without the application through physical life.

Question 15

Anne:–I am not sure if you understood my question of perpetuation. What I wanted to know was if God was still in perpetuation, is He still sending forth the sparks of Himself which are our spirit, and will this continue through all time?

Red Feather:–Yes. It is never-ending. The experience from the beginning has to be gone through for those who are still in darkness (ignorance). They have that spark within them but they do not as yet recognise it; therefore, God will send them greater and greater help to get that recognition to give the perpetuation its affinity purpose and then the soul becomes freer.

The spark will be kept alive, the spark will continually be refurbished until there comes a point when that spark will burst forth into a little flame and enough light (knowledge) is generated to give that spirit perpetuation and purpose.

Anne:–How does thought come into our minds so that we hear it within? What actually is thought?

Red Feather:–Thought is activated spirit, be it your own or from another source. Thoughts can be sent to you by those of us who love you within the spirit realms, those who wish to teach you, those who wish to guide you.

You can receive those thoughts as a pure clear message. Other thoughts will be slightly blurred and you are unsure of their full content and meaning.

The other way you receive thought is from your higher self – those thoughts should be the clearest of them all and be the directive type of thought. We cannot direct you, we can only place a suggestion and trust that you will pick it up, only the higher self has the right to direct you.

Watch your thoughts, see which are directive, which are suggestions, then you will be able to fathom out for yourself just where they come from.

The directive ones, I repeat, are always from your own higher self for only it has the right to direct you. The suggestions for a course of action come from us – suggested lines of thought rather than factual thought, they are much broader based and give a broad spectrum of action to choose from.

The loving thoughts of kindness, of family, are either from yourself or from members of your own family in spirit because through the ties of family love they have the strongest link with you and is where they are able to influence you. Family thought can be very strong if based on family love, they have an impetus to communicate through genuine concern for family well-being and an established line of communication built up during earthly life – love is never lost and is the strongest and truest force for good.

It pays to analyse your thoughts, categorise them and you will see from that how much you are influenced from spirit, from yourself, and from others who wish you to progress.

Anne:–What of negative thought, impure thought?

Red Feather:–This usually comes to you from your own physical mind and its lack of understanding; the subconscious area where you have been presented with a situation in which the line of communication from your higher self is not clear – it is a fudged area and you are not sure how to react; because it is physical mind the negative – the line of least understanding – is the one it follows.

Usually you will find with negative thought that it stirs around for a long time until eventually a little further knowledge sheds light on to the situation and greater understanding results. The struggle of the physical mind to take into itself the higher self-thinking to understand what is right from what is wrong.

Anne:–Within the higher self is contained all the knowledge gleaned from our previous lives. Many of those experiences have been both negative and impure, nor can they have yet been worked out for they still remain – is this not how a lot of these thoughts come to us?

Red Feather:–You are forgetting one aspect of this – the higher self has greater scope than the physical self for seeing the causes and results of thought. Although it may have taken to itself a past experience which caused negative thoughts, the higher self can always see the result of that negative thought and will struggle against that result. It will go towards what is good, this is what causes great repercussions in those who think deeply. It can cause great repercussions in physical life because it is not understood.

The higher self sees through the hindsight of previous experience and is not fettered by physical thinking; it still has access to its whole understanding to that point whereas the physical self is only a facet of that whole and complete understanding is not within it.

Some negative thoughts are not impure. Seen from spirit – they are in the process of being worked through and are taken into the physical subconscious to be further worked through, but always with the support of the higher self who can see further, deeper, and know better, because it knows more purely.

There are negative aspects within all – there has to be for we are not yet pure, but this does not mean that you cannot gain from a negative aspect. Working through negative aspects towards their greater understanding dilutes the negative and eventually turns it into a positive aspect – correct application of knowledge gained.

Anne:–This is a question about my development. I thought it might be helpful to ask, because other people may experience the same sort of things, could you explain why I experience the tremendous weight upon my head, the heart within my body and the electrical type shock waves when I am in meditation?

Red Feather:–The simple answer is that you are not in harmony with the vibrations which surround you. The more in harmony the spirit self is with its higher self and its God, the more it seeks to bring into line that harmony within the physical senses and understanding.

Let me illustrate. Spirit is the sea, you are a diver and must go down to a wreck on the bottom of the sea. As you go through the varying depths of the water you require pressurising to keep harmony of the physical body so that no distress is caused. When distress occurs the diver gets the condition known as the bends, he has to be brought to the surface and receive oxygen.

The sea is representative of the rate of vibration around you, the wreck at the bottom of the sea – your hidden treasure of inner truth of the spirit self. The distance to be covered is the rate of disharmony between the spirit self and the physical expression of that self.

You have done enough research and are positive the treasure is there. You have trained for this dive as best you can without getting into the sea, you have prepared yourself to reach the wreck but you have only had practise dives at different levels within the sea.

The first ones held in shallow water were easy but as you practise in deeper water the pressure has to be adjusted, those controlling the air valves and such things from the shore – liken to us in spirit – the deeper you go the more we must adjust so that in safety you can go deeper still.

We capture your resolve to give all you have to get there and we give all we can to help you but your physical body has limitations which you have overlooked. What you want to do is plunge straight down without a diving-suit – we cannot allow this as it would cause you harm.

We must take you gradually to depths which are safe; as you go deeper the disharmony and the pressure begins to change, subtle variations are noted. We are adjusting to your new thoughts and the metabolism within your body to allow you to dive in safety to reach that treasure you know is there.

When you dive very occasionally you are able to bring up some of that treasure, albeit only from the top. This makes you more keen and impatient to reach those deeper levels so beneficial to you. Try if you can to make you diving purposeful in this way – see the treasure trove from where you stand, mark it and proceed towards it at an even pace. You are apt sometimes to jump in feet first, sometimes head first, without waiting to assess the surrounding currents.

Take hold of the safety line of your natural vibration rate then ease yourself into the water, get used to the vibrations around you and let them take you gently down towards the treasure.

Your physical body and thoughts play a part in the vibrations that surround you. By your very nature you delve into matters which give interest but you have not come to any real conclusion as whether to throw out or accept the thoughts which come into your mind. You feel you need more tangible facts before you can proceed with this inner journey.

It is so much more complex than you can realise, we are all much more complex beings than is realised. The very food eaten affects the vibrations, there are negative foods to eat as there are negative thoughts to think.

In every aspect of your life there is an effect on the vibrations around you and we help you deal with those vibrations which can change a dozen times a day so that you can reach your treasure in safety. The elements also play a part, everything you touch or touches you within the earth plane affects the vibration rates surrounding you; dull, heavy, static weather makes energy more difficult to work through while clear, crisp, bright weather gives an easy flow.

It is a matter of degree how easily you blend with all that surrounds you, how deeply you dive into the inner reaches of the self. Put physical life in its proper perspective of being only a moment in eternity and the physical mind blockages to spiritual progress melt away resulting in greater harmony of the spirit and its expression.

The uncomfortable pressures you experience during meditation are the effects of the disharmony between the spirit self and the physical mind blockages. You cannot force the pace of your progression it must be a natural occurrence, a natural balance of the vibrations within the body, mind and soul. Delve, understand, accept or reject, taking one step at a time; build knowledge a little at a time securing the foundations ever deeper in truth. This it the way forward, little by little, and not by taking one single deep dive in an uncontrolled state of impatience. Control of the self within is the answer, when this is gained truth yields its knowledge.

Question 16

Doreen:–Sometimes when working with colour I have difficulty in distinguishing between indigo and black.

Red Feather:–If the colour is indigo there will be a feeling of life and stretchability in it. If it is black it will be solid and non-giving.

Doreen:–Also, I often see what I call my silver paper colours. Can you explain what connection, if any, these have?

Red Feather:–Silver outbursts, the opening of your inspiration and receptivity to spirit. The silver thread of knowledge which YOU take into understanding from the gold of pure spirit and use as part of your individuality.

When you see gold and silver know that the gold is original spirit, original truth and wisdom whilst the silver represents your understanding and working towards the truth and your acceptance of knowledge to this point in your evolution.

Joy:–Could you explain how I will use inspirational reading exercises, since this work is to be done by Doreen. What point, therefore, in my doing them as well?

Red Feather:–First of all they are a way to allow me to bring greater expression through you. In the future the real reason will be to enable you to asses the amount of freedom that each soul has gained for itself and how much it can safely gain for itself through the teaching you will be able to give, or the group can give.

It is an assessment of freedom and purpose, of how the soul has reached that point and how it can go forward. The application of the colours to each other will be of importance to you – the balance between past and present for their future trends. These readings are an account balance sheet for you to decide the teaching routine that will be best for them.

Doreen:–How will painting come to play a part in my future work?

Red Feather:–Through your love of nature you will be able to illustrate the inner self in a way which can be understood. It is no use confusing the investigators with terminology they cannot understand. What we are going to do, therefore, is use your love of nature as something to which they can respond – like a flower or an animal and through this you will show their individual expansion first in a general way and then in a more detailed way.

The soul is something which is difficult to relate to, an abstract form they know is there and yet cannot imagine, it is too vast. They need to have their interest pin-pointed in a way that they can both understand and relate to. Their response to your illustration of nature's beauty in the little animal or flower will show them the beauty and the purpose in the evolution of the individual soul.

Anne:–The physical body is nothing (earth is a part of the spirit realm) – yet we need it – why is it so important?

Red Feather:–The point of physical life is to gain experience through refinement for the spirit self. You have your higher self which understands more of spirit and its responsibilities than your physical mind does at the moment. That higher self has to test its knowledge through practical expression.

When you come to earth you do so in a physical body with a physical mind which is not so enlarged as your spirit self and is then confined to a particular degree of self knowledge which sets aside its full recognition of the whole self. In this situation the spirit in the physical body is directed along paths of many experiences to gain a little from each towards a more rounded expansion for the whole self.

Physical life is merely a vehicle to get you from A to B, physical life gives to the spirit self a conveyance for opportunity and a gaining from that opportunity to expand the spirit self. Therefore, what are you? You are a contained spirit on a journey to greater expansion with no signposts directly given, no road map or route planned for you other than the amount of information which your own higher self can give to you. You hold the route map – your own life pattern – you planned it before you came into the confines of physical life and by your own thoughts and actions will you reap the result of progress made upon the earth.

Anne:–This question is about negative thought forms which come via the physical mind, even though one knows one has a higher self and is spirit, this causes confusion.

Red Feather:–When you break new ground your spade takes up many weeds and cells of weeds from under the ground where they lay hidden from sight. Through digging you expose them to air and sight. You then have to bend down to remove each of the weeds to get clean earth before you use it for growing plants; however, as those plants show through so do more weeds. Likewise your mind and its thoughts, for as you come to understand spirit and its progressive working you are even more aware of the need for refinement. The journey to the inner self is made through the conquering of the many layers of negative influences which are strewn on the pathway of life and only by recognising their presence and dealing with them can refinement of spirit take place.

Doreen:–All things have an aura. The other evening I asked to be shown auras of both people and animals. The auras of the animals were different in appearance and I seemed to notice a split about the centre, was I correct, I was a little unsure?

Red Feather:–With animals you must be careful to categorise those which have been touched by man – been caused to respond to man either through fear or love for they will have a different aura to those animals untouched by man. Animals expectation and understanding of life is very different to that of man in that there is no cognizant pattern of understanding which can be followed – it is limited in that instinct rules above reason.

Pets or animals which have been loved and/or trained by man and have given their limited love to man are expanded through that contact with man; therefore their auras will be more recognisable and like to that of a human – because love is the operating factor.

The reverse of this are animals who have cause to fear through contact with man and been driven through fear, grown up or experienced fear in some form. Their auras will be very, very contracted, misshapen, under-developed, because they have not received the balance of love within their lives to give them a rounded aura.

All mankind, all animals in contact with man who have known love, have an expanded love vibration to aid their progression. Those animals who have only known fear in their lives have never experienced the love vibration to give them that expansion.

The animals which are used just for breeding without any expression of love or any conscious feeling of love shown to them also have a limited aura. The division you saw was this particular contraction – the lack of love vibration.

Without the love vibration they do not have sufficient strength within them to sustain a separate identity and progress on to higher individuality. They form a species group and take on the aura of the group whole.

All animals which receive love from man and give love to man are on the love vibration which leads them to higher understanding, higher intellect within themselves and they can therefore retain personality for a much longer period of time.

Anne:–I was wondering about the male/female division. Each spirit having polarities, do we consist of both? Do we sometimes come forth as man and sometimes as woman?

Red Feather:–The simple answer is yes. The timing of that will depend upon the ultimate aim of experience which that particular gender requires to develop in that particular facet of itself. If you should come to earth with the intent of experiencing motherhood and through some fault either of your mate or of circumstances you cannot have children, then you would come forth again in another life as woman to experience motherhood.

It is the same question of polarity. The male strength and the female strength are different but give to each other what the other requires to be whole. As you are a whole so you must have all experiences and must develop within yourself both strengths – this takes time.

Man and woman are complex characters; they have within the same gender different strengths to be experienced. A man can be brave, cowardly, gentle, harsh, and has to learn to temper these things in moderation for the common good and then to lift that moderation to the higher experience of spiritual love and service.

The woman must do the same. She has within her the strength and gentleness of motherhood, she has within a caring to establish a home, a safe base from which to view the world, change the world at family level; this has to be heightened to the highest level of universal love and motherhood.

Within all these strengths many are common to both, i.e. the love of beauty, the love of music and the arts, etc. as seen from a man's point of view, may be very different from that of a woman.

There are different aspects of the human personality which are better developed in either one sex or the other. Ultimately you will have balance using the best from the male and female strengths you have gathered, but you must strive towards that balance very gently, very slowly.

Question 17

Anne:–I was reading a book the other day which, if I understood it right, said that when spirit came forth, it came having both male and female attributes, but these separated, becoming duality and that only at some future enlightened stage in evolution would they again become joined.

Red Feather:–While it is true that you have within yourself female and male counterparts – even as you are now female, there are strains that are masculine in tendency which your particular strength of femaleness requires. It is a bringing about of the whole. Each advancement of spiritual understanding brings an evening out of the male and female genders within each, whether you are male or female. This is brought about very slowly over a long period so that you gain an equal understanding of both the male and female facets within yourself.

All work towards this oneness in God; it is all part of the ongoing search for spirit progression. As you live life upon earth you are more aware of the attributes of male and female. There must be a coming together and this will happen as people progress along their spiritual pathway. In some men there is a great gentleness of a female nature, likewise in a woman great gentleness of a male. They have rounded and advanced their personality, taking both within themselves, but it must be expanded further still.

Within each individual there are male and female traits. These traits must be strengthened to give the spirit self its own propulsion towards even greater purity within God. Let me now take you to a time when you will be much further progressed spirits, much further progressed than you can at this time understand; I, too, will be further progressed and at that time individuality will not longer satisfy. Then there is merging, but only when individuality no longer satisfies. It is then not a case of male and female, it is a case of unity in balance.

Anne:–I also read that our teachers, our guides, can come forth to us in different guises for different reasons using different vibrations.

Red Feather:–Yes, go on.

Anne:–Well, I was wondering, are you and the "The Director" one, are you in fact all people (spirit) who come through Joy? (Joy says Red Feather is grinning at you Anne, he's teasing.)

Red Feather:–NO, I am not all the personalities who manifest through Joy, I reject that completely – if you use your own common sense and go over all the speeches that have been given you will find different personality facets.

I am the teacher of you all but I am not the only teacher. It is true and I will concede that I am not known as Red Feather, but I will not concede to being "The Director".

As you have different personalities within yourself – those shown in your various incarnations, am I not also allowed the same freedom? I have facets which match your own, your training, your need and God's need for our dual purpose, therefore, as you incarnate into one facet, so I match it with the exact one needed from spirit.

In this case I am a teacher and Joy my mouthpiece – we are both teachers, we have been other things but always the one is matched which the other. Basically we will always be teachers that is the role in which we are happiest, that is the role in which we fulfil our best potential. Others who will come through Joy will not always be used as teachers. There are those who come through as healers, like Silver Dove who works with Mary. He will teach, but it is through healing that he will teach, he will use his instrument in the way he can use her best: likewise, White Cloud will use you for inspirational writing as well as for other things. It is also true I give interpretation for Doreen's work as her interpretation is not yet able to function, when her teachers are able to bring it forth you will find a distinct difference between the two leaving no doubt that some other facet of some other person is at work – not me.

Anne:–I am sorry, I did not mean to say that you were Silver Dove, or Father Godfrey, or White Cloud, but that as stated by you – in different incarnations you have come through Joy as different personalities, now in your more advanced position – are you not able to bring forth those different personalities through the varying stages of consciousness?

Red Feather:–This is not needed, those personalities brought forth before have been superseded by this facet.

Anne:–So, do you only come through Joy as the person we know as Red Feather?

Red Feather:–Yes, for the moment. My medium trusts me as Red Feather. I must remain constant, she knows me so well that if I were to confuse her with other vibrations – which she could recognise as mine – it would build up doubt within her mind and this I cannot afford. Therefore, I am as Red Feather and will be as Red Feather – until a later date.

Question 18

Anne:–During the time the circle was closed Doreen and I were asked why spirit had to be tried and tested. The answer we gave did not satisfy so we got to thinking about it – this is what we came up with, your comments would be appreciated. We do realise that this answer could be entirely wrong, please bear with us as it is rather lengthy.

The Great Spirit (God) is the whole and contains all there is – therefore both the positive and the negative aspects of all, God and the devil as it came to be understood, a tremendous power of light and darkness, a constructive and destructive power – if both were equally balanced, but should the negative aspect grow and get the upper hand it could destroy the whole, i.e. such as atomic power wrongly utilised, only more so – it's a possibility. Was this how spirit came to be tried and tested – portions of the great spirit individualising to work and strengthen the positive in all aspects through all experiences, eventually bringing about a balance of positive/positive instead of positive/negative to the whole?

Now I would come to the affinity, the main affinity line, to colour and music, i.e. vibrational harmony. If the Great Spirit divided itself into different portions, each portion containing all aspects, all colours, all notes of vibration to cover all experiences, but each portion having as its main colour, its main strength, its main pathway, i.e. the Golden

Road, the Blue Road, etc., then did each of these portions individualise into different degrees – i.e. the main affinity line, thereby in reality all degrees of each affinity line are one, having come from the same portion of the Great Spirit, each degree responsible for overcoming the negative aspect of its own individuality so that the positive, the strength, the light of the whole is increased.

Earth is a duplicate of Spirit – similar but not the same, it is darker, more dense, with slower vibrations with great negativity. Spirit veiled in human form – its vehicle of the body to give its expression, must work harder to overcome the negative aspects (strengthened continually from its source via its group soul, i.e. the affinity line, to do so).

In time in the forseeable future as all negative aspects are changed into first weak positives, then in balanced positives, so will the earth become lighter, more in tune, the veil will crumble and fall away. Each colour becoming paler and paler as it loses more and more of its negative aspects until once again it becomes the white of the Divine origin. So does the shade of colour, the depth of colour, the brightness of colour show the degree travelled from negative towards positive? This then, Red Feather, a theory, would you be kind enough to comment.

Red Feather:–I congratulate you on some very positive thinking and reasoning. The basis is correct insofar as you go with it – there are certain words I would rather you did not use, i.e. "division", but insofar as knowledge has been given to you, you have used it well in answering this complex question.

About the balance I would make correction – it is not an equal balance of good and bad, negative/positive, for there is always more good than bad in any situation – it is the finding of it that is difficult. Where there is on earth at any one time a situation which appears to be for the worse, more negative than positive, always is provided compensatory good aspects, positive aspects within the surrounding area to make the negative less viable. In any situation, be it personal, national, or a world situation – this applies.

At no time is the division between good and evil equal, it always favours the good, the positive, because the negative comes from the misunderstood positive use, therefore – as it was positive to begin with the negative much less. The favour is about two thirds and one third. Where the good can only get better, more strong, the negative can only get weaker – this is another difference you must allow for. It may not always be apparent but it is always so.

The appearance of negative winning over positive is this misunderstood absorption of the extra ingredients from Spirit to compensate the heavily negative atmosphere and until that extra is absorbed it will appear that the negative is winning – but it is not the case. Positive aspects cannot be infiltrated quickly into a black negative situation because that would then upset the balance too quickly, and realisation of what the negative is doing does not occur – therefore good does not come from it, only continued ignorance.

I understand that this is very difficult for man to grasp – man would like all negative aspects immediately removed so that everyone could have it better there and then, but if that was done it would be a temporary gain only because people would think – here we have a very bad situation in the world yet it came right very quickly, therefore we are free to do it again – and again. Man himself must realise that he is in a negative situation, accept the positive help which is there and activate for good – activation is what turns the negative into the positive and this you will understand takes time.

Earth is the proving ground from the negative to the positive; it is where realisation dawns and having dawned is put into practice. Very tentatively that realisation is grown upon to become positive aspects within life contributing to the good of all mankind. Earth was created to be this proving ground – that is why it is there – that is why people come forth from spirit in such great numbers to help man understand his own negative aspects and how they can be changed.

Earth is your kindergarten – it is not real life, it never has been – it is only a facet of whole life. Because life is so complicated it cannot be experienced and fulfilled within one earthly lifetime. If I were to tell you how tiny, microcosmic in relation to the whole is this little speck of dust which is the earth you would come to understand how all purity cannot be achieved within a designated span of earth years for the negativity based in the earth must be changed from that speck of dust into firstly a little glimmer of positive light, then more so.

It will do this, but it all takes a great deal of time. It takes all of us time, even in the spirit world it takes time for the realisation to dawn that the spirit being can only progress by understanding and correcting his own negativity/ignorance.

Hardship will happen, it will occur by the very nature of the earth's planetary influences. It is no mistake that the earth was placed where it is between the planets because planetary draw has a great influence upon the spheres which surround it and are adjacent to it. The planets are ranged around your earth and in your cosmos in a particular fashion each one representing a different style, a different aspect of the Great Spirit. Life is different on all of them, the lessons are different, but you need them all and you must go through them all before you can begin to understand what the Great Spirit actually is.

Your troubles on earth – and there are many – may seem to you like the end of the world, that God does not exist because there are so many hardships, so many crimes against the person, but it is a necessary lesson in your own evolvement as spirit to refrain from that which can be abused, that which is horrific, to turn towards something positive and good so that you can feel strength from that positivity instead of revulsion of the negative. When you do that then you are progressing as spirit, you are contributing towards the strength of the whole which surrounds your own planet, which surrounds your whole cosmos, because even though you are a little speck you contribute to the whole cosmos.

Your thoughts are important, little or deep thoughts placed in the correct dimension with sincerity and love of God, with understanding for your fellow men, all contribute to the good within your whole earth. People often say – "why does God not do this, why can He not change that, God does not exist at all, He allows so much which is not conversant with love of mankind." My children – YOU are the ones who can change that for God exists in you; your own thoughts can change it, because as I have stated you contribute to the positive aspects on your earth, therefore – you can change the conditions in which you live.

It is hard for man to grasp this because he thinks of himself as a physical being whereas in fact, he is of spirit and spirit being so much stronger than the physical why then should he not be able to effect the spiritual evolvement of his own planet? As you change that around yourself you contribute to the ether around the earth so the earth benefits as well as yourself. You cannot separate the two, it is not possible.

Let me deal with the divisions as you call them. I dislike the word "divisions". There is no division, there was no division. It is difficult to explain in earthly terms what actually happened. Let me try, but remember that my explanation is not sufficient, it is merely to give you an idea. It was more a 'lending' than a division. The whole lent itself but was still whole within itself, no portion of it taken out from the whole and solely used for one particular aspect. There was a lending of the whole towards understanding – degrees of understanding – but it was still all the whole.

The whole is to us a much wider concept than it is to you. The whole of the Great Spirit cannot be divided in any way because each part of the whole spirit is the whole part. There are not little sections, it is always the perfect whole and that perfect whole lends itself to whatever degree of understanding is required. It is the degree of understanding which separates. Let me go further. In the degrees and affinities of which you speak they are likened to the scales of music, higher and lower degrees of that same understanding. The whole spirit is in each of that understanding complete as to recipient's understanding but within even the lower scale there is the same amount of understanding as in the higher one – it is he who plays the scale who picks his own tune. As within a scale of music you can use a variety of notes, so can you in understanding, that is why the whole is in each of the scales. As a pianist becomes more proficient he is able to mix the scales better to play upon the whole piano keyboard – so it is with understanding and degrees of understanding.

The lesser degree of understanding is no way less complete than the very high, it is the competence of the player that determines the division of understanding. As you become more proficient at playing the piano so a player can join with others who can play different instruments to perform first as small group, later an orchestra, then a choral group with it, perhaps all of them playing their own part to provide a united whole in harmony yet each of them doing their own particular thing within the whole.

So it is with spiritual understanding and with different degrees of different understandings; you have some people who sing, some people who play an instrument, each is necessary to the whole and because each plays his part to perfection the whole is strengthened, if one drops out it is weakened. This can be compensated for by the others as long as too many do not drop out if that should happen there would be a negative slide in understanding – this sometimes happens in your world.

It happened in your dark ages where positive thinking in your world was actually dampened by conditions surrounding it, unfortunately brought about by the church people, but that is lightened now, people are beginning to practice their own scales of understanding. No longer do they wish to listen to someone else's harmony they wish to find their own. Your world is emerging into a strength situation which will become apparent in the middle of the next century. You are emerging from your own darkness beginning to feel your own scales of understanding within God the Father, within the whole; your own purpose in being within that whole and what you can contribute to others. It is a slow process, the degrees must work slowly to gain insight and harmony.

Anne:–I was wondering if I was right about the cores, the core being the main service pathway surrounded then by all the other colours in lesser degree, for each must all go through all experiences, i.e. like your piano player, the piano his main instrument yet he could also play other instruments to a satisfactory level, but not as well as he plays the piano.

Red Feather:–Each of you has your own strengths and degrees of affinity to work along. Those degrees of affinity are in harmony. You have found within your own group a harmonious vibration and you can all work within it. If you were to leave and join another group things might not work out as well that does not mean to say that your affinity or theirs is wrong, simply that they are different. The end result would be the same in a heightened consciousness in your world though the way of getting there would inevitably be different.

As to the colours of the core to which you refer, I do not feel at this time that I want to go into them as deeply as is implicated because you do not yet understand colour as fully as I wish. Colour is an affinity in its own right, and as it has graduations of knowledge and you must work through them to gain in understanding.

Question 19

Anne:–I would ask about natural psychics some of whom do not know what it is that confronts them. This sometimes leads to fear, is then talked about in such a way that others are frightened away from having dealings with this great truth. What part has this to play, why does it come forth thus?

Red Feather:–You are speaking again about degrees of the affinity line, degrees of understanding. There are occasions when you have noticed talent which is unharnessed, unprofessional – so it is with psychics. It is that the ability is apparent and uppermost as opposed to its understanding and control. It is the inconsistent working of the higher self with the lower self where the channel is clear but no harnessed understanding comes through. Where the ability manifests in one way or another as in vision or in hearing, harnesses itself to the projection so well but understanding is limited therefore a negative aspect of that understanding is taken. It is, if you will, as someone who can read reasonably well, who can enjoy and understand a novel but for whom a work of Einstein's would be lost because of the lack of its understanding. Therefore something which is not understood but the power felt, seen or heard is then experienced. The power causes the fear because it is uncontrolled and not understood making the human mind fearful.

Anne:–Yes, it does, but I think it is sad that this experience tends to put people off, they are afraid of that which needs to be taught to them.

Red Feather:–It may frighten them but it also makes them think. Consider – if you had upon your earth psychics or spiritual exponents who always used harnessed power and understood the power clearly you would have others say – 'I needn't bother because I cannot do it and why should I try for I have no need of it in my life.' But if you have people with unharnessed power who still operate within a visual or a hearing capacity – it makes doubters think. They have not consciously tried to develop this and is an experience they don't even want half of the time – yet it comes, what is it?

Everything has its own part to play. Those who have unharnessed power have responsibility upon them to harness that power, but in the gaining of that responsibility they cause others to think on the origin of that unharnessed power, therefore it is not lost.

Anne:–What about the very elderly who begin to suddenly see and hear, who are frightened by it, not having had the experience before?

Red Feather:–This is a gradual process, a bridging between the two worlds so that consciousness can adjust. As people approach near the end of their lives it can happen that vistas open up before them of the world that is to be to allow conscious understanding to adjust to the fact that life after death is reality.

May I take you back to the original question which sparked off all this thinking. Why did spirit have to be tried and tested? Why does a baby grow to adulthood – it is to experience through growing consciousness – that is the simple answer. However, I do realise that this answer is too simple; let me elaborate by going back to nature. Let us take a pear tree. It begins as a seed which is planted into fertile soil, you nourish and look after it. The seed then grows into a young plant, a sapling, then a young tree and finally a fully mature tree bearing fruit in its own right – regeneration.

God must regenerate to gain strength, goodness and love into all that there is so that all can perpetuate. As a baby comes into this world you see it in its innocence and beauty. As you watch it begins to respond, smile, try to reach forward, later it will begin to crawl and then it will walk and talk. This child is now a toddler and curious about everything but some of the things it reaches for are not safe, like hot fires, substances that can poison, etc. Those around that child must make sure that its environment is kept safe until the time that the child can take the responsibility for its own environment.

The regeneration of man in God's own image man has to do the same type of thing. He has to learn simply to be born in the sight of God and in God's image. This can take place at any age, not just a babe and there are many people upon the earth who live their whole lives without the realisation that they are born in God's image. All the time the Spirit of God within works towards this feeling of being a child in the image of God for however long it takes. Then the child must learn to walk in God's image, to walk with God's love for himself, mankind, and all that is within his sphere. It takes time for man to walk with God.

God regenerates and regenerates His own image time and time again until the realisation dawns that all, ALL is within God's image. When that happens the spirit becomes stronger and along the way are not tests but little experiences to probe the spirit within towards that God feeling, bringing it to a recognition that it has indeed been moulded in God's own image. Experiences of an adverse kind which happen to you through your own decisions help you to learn to walk more with God that previously; you have learnt what is within God's image and what is not, what is therefore right for you and what is not – the positive and the negative.

On the other hand you may do something you may not consider to be very much but was needed by someone else; this leaves you with a feeling of great love and satisfaction and you feel a better person because of it. This is the God image flowering within you. It is a gradual process and cannot be quickened more than the understanding of the image of God within you is understood.

If the full image of God were to be unleashed upon your physical mind without previous understanding you could not begin to comprehend the greatness, therefore would it be dismissed. But little by little the growing awareness comes, the growing direction comes, the flowering of God within comes until it is a strength which no longer can be denied. It happens at different rates for different people but know always that it will happen . . . No one can gain it for anyone else because the image of God within you is for you and you alone – thus is your spirit tried and tested.

Anne:–Can you explain the apparent cruelty found within the animal kingdom?

Red Feather:–Animals do not have reasoning consciousness but as they come closer and closer to and more involved with man and his love giving so consciousness establishes itself more deeply. Therefore a cat will learn not to scratch those who look after it if it is well treated, a dog does not bite when it learns to trust those around it.

Animals in the wild have survival consciousness only for their own species. Domesticated animals begin to have reasoning consciousness which leads to higher evolution for them and the whole.

Question 20

Anne:–I ask about the diamond spoken of so often by Silver Birch. Is each facet of that diamond representative of a colour, one or two facets coming forth at a time to try and reach its next potential of degree so going round the facets until that degree is completed? Would the space between the base and the apex of that diamond represent our potential of full enlightenment?

Red Feather:–The diamond as spoken of by Silver Birch was the facet of the person as a whole. Silver Birch was generalising to make it understandable.

The diamond can be used in many ways. I use the diamond as each individual, higher and lower self together. Each facet of that diamond is an expression of the positive strength or the weakness of that person. Where it is placed upon the diamond shows where the weakness lies, i.e. the upper half in the spiritual, the lower in the physical self.

Each facet is an expression of the self. Look at the various expressions you can have on any one topic and you will see the need for the different glints of the diamond. For any one topic you can have positive and negative thoughts, therefore each facet is also diamond shaped; where it originates in the true positive sense it is in the upper half, in the negative it is in the lower. Watch then where it is placed within the whole diamond and you will see where it needs to gather its strength or its expression.

The spirit which stands represented by the whole diamond shows where you have gained strength from previous weakness. If you had eyes to see you would note that the facets of the diamond are never still – they move constantly according to your thoughts, your actions and gained experiences. They move place, they can be transferred from the lower to the higher, and once gained into the higher never do they lose their colour or their texture, but they can then go on to the centre of the diamond to become purer, harder and part of the whole core.

That core of the diamond is the spark of God which He gave to you, that part of Himself which is within you. The very centre of that diamond is immovable, it is pure, but all the facets surrounding it are movable.

As you incarnate into the earth for experience you use the facets on the outer side of your diamond. All experiences which you go through are then transferred to one of the inner layers if you have gained from them, if you have not and have lost the lesson of that experience they remain on the outer shell, yet to be strengthened, yet to be removed. It is like the degrees of consciousness, the degrees of attainment, you can move up and down, inwards and up or down, depending upon your own reaction and acceptance of the experience before you. All of you have your own polarities to seek, to bring into balance.

As in the material world jewellers can fashion you diamonds into many shapes – a small top with a big base, the other way around, and many other shapes in between, so you shape your own diamond. Whilst upon the earth never do you have the perfect diamond shape – you cannot, for you are still trying to work out the weaknesses to strengthen them. Whatever shape your diamond is that same core is always in the centre. The strength is there to lend to the weakness outside.

If you reflect upon a diamond in your material world the beauty of it comes from the centre, that's what gives it it's depth and it's brilliance – so too with you. The more you can give true expression of God to your core, from your core to the outer limits of your diamond, so shall you shine with the brilliance and the depth of the true diamond of your world.

Take a facet of your diamond on the outer edges about the mid way line – you have within that the top of it touching the spiritual but most of it embedded in the physical world and the physical life references. How can this be changed – perhaps someone you love hurts you, deeply hurts you, you can have two reactions. Sorrow that you have been hurt yet a continuing love for that person, or you can have bitterness within your heart, those two reactions will lead you in different ways. The first way strengthens you because you give understanding and continued love to the one who has caused you hurt, therefore you gain from your understanding, you feel a deeper and more involved love for that person.

If you have bitterness in your heart you see only the negative side of that person, you harbour negative thoughts towards yourself. In doing this your diamond becomes more brittle, you become more brittle, it is sharper, as you become more sharp in your reaction to them. Now a sharper diamond can go down more deeply, so it is with your negative facet and it embeds itself deeper into the physical but with the reverse positive reaction – love is light, love is understanding and compassionate, it expands itself and its knowledge of itself because of this, therefore it lifts itself and can then become part of the higher section – the spiritual section of your own self. This is but one example of how you yourselves shape your own diamond.

To give another example on a wider scale – your reaction to world poverty, to the horrific things that go on in your world; you can react to them with compassion but worst of all you can be disinterested. Never let it be thought that you need to have a definite action or reaction to bring about a negative result in some cases complete disinterest brings about a much worse effect than that of anger or hatred. Anger and hatred cool, can be replaced with knowledge into enlightenment, disinterest is asleep and first has to be awakened and this means a longer route to enlightenment.

I wish to bring another example to you. Little children have to be taught and given certain standards to live their lives by, these are given by those who are responsible for them. You also have to live by certain rules and standards and you were given those at the moment God breathed His spark into you. They have been there from the beginning so no one can turn round and say that he/she was unaware of this for those instructions have already been given. What you have to do is to uncover them and put them into practice. When you come to see yourself as you really are you cannot have the excuse that you did not know, you only have the excuse you did not seek to find.

By not seeking to find you create a negative aspect to your self. Try to encourage those who come to you to seek themselves, so that they will be able to say – 'I did try, perhaps I did not find, but I did try.' Because after your teaching and your explanations they say – 'I am sorry I did not know I had to seek myself' – then you will have failed, we will have failed, but most of all the person will have lost the opportunity to find himself, and his failure adds a little to your own negativity because you did not carry out your task to the best of your ability.

I hear you say – 'Surely their responsibility to search is upon themselves, we cannot do that for them.' This is true up to a point, it IS their ultimate responsibility, but it is your responsibility to put the way there before them in a way they cannot refuse to seek into themselves. I lay at your feet a great responsibility but be mindful that you do not walk this way alone, we are there, we shall give to you exactly what is needed, therefore give expression to what we give to you and never will you be able to stand beside someone who says – because of your teaching I did not know I had to look into myself.

Build your own diamond in its own perfection. It is there in all its beauty and all its original perfection greatly strengthened, but also weakened by your own inability to understand. Everyone has this problem, everyone has to come to terms with the shape of diamond they have built for themselves. Build now for an even diamond, for a balanced diamond, for a glowing, living diamond. Let your diamond be one that is used to drill into the depth of those who seek, not simply one which lies upon a shelf and just beautifies without doing anything. You have been given working tips to your diamond, so drill well, drill long and drill hard, and in that way you strengthen your own facet – every facet of your own diamond.